WHY WE MARCH

WHY WE MARCH

Straight Answers

NADINE FORBES

iUniverse, Inc.
New York Lincoln Shanghai

Why We March
Straight Answers

iUniverse books may be ordered through booksellers or by contacting:

iUniverse
2021 Pine Lake Road, Suite 100
Lincoln, NE 68512
www.iuniverse.com
1-800-Authors (1-800-288-4677)

Because of the dynamic nature of the Internet, any Web addresses or links contained in this book may have changed since publication and may no longer be valid.

ISBN: 978-0-595-45696-3 (pbk)
ISBN: 978-0-595-89998-2 (ebk)

Printed in the United States of America

Contents

1

Here We Are

Several years ago I was reading a powerful book by Stephen Covey titled *The 7 Habits of Highly Effective People* and I came across a quote that changed my life: "Seek first to understand, then be understood."[1] Mr. Covey and I are in agreement that so many people spend a disproportionate amount of time speaking and not enough time listening. We also spend too little time inquiring and too much time judging without adequate understanding. We attach ourselves unfortunately to the status quo because it is effortless; right or wrong.

If haven't tasted fresh clean water, we will continuously drink unclean water to quench our thirst. In that I mean we thirst for many things. We thirst for power, we thirst for acceptance, and we search for understanding. If we observe a behavior, inappropriate or not, that leads to power and acceptance, that behavior is what will quench our thirst for those desires, and that behavior is what will be emulated. If fed misinformation as an explanation of what is foreign or different to us, unfortunately that is what quenches our thirst for understanding, until otherwise convinced.

For generations the general public has been figurative handed a tall glass of prejudice, being brainwashed that different expression of affection, namely homosexuality, is perverted and criminal in nature. Consequentially, homosexuals have been an oppressed group and targets of hatred. As attitudes toward homosexuals change, more heterosexuals are becoming sympathetic to our fight for rights and civil liberties. Other heterosexuals though are still influenced by false information or are blinded by lack of information. In order to engage in an intelligent dialog on the subject of homosexuality you need to moderately, if not fully, understand what homosexuality is without the assumptive "I know it all" attitude or by approaching the issue with negative preconceived notions. Distain and disgust towards a group of people based on stereotype and misconception is not only asinine but has potentially serious consequence on society as a whole.

Before determining what is right and wrong, one must revisit the history of previous assumptions of right and wrong. What is deemed wrong may simply be different or outside the norm; no need for condemnation. Before judging what is inappropriate, one needs to look at what is deemed the same in their privileged lives. Before using the Bible, one should thoroughly read the Bible as well as study the translations of the Bible; not just selected convenient passages. Lastly, before accusing a group of crimes or being unfit, one must devote some time in doing comparative research and analyzing crime and social statistics. That is only intelligent.

Homosexuality is not wrong. Homosexuality is, though, uncommon, in that, of the six billion souls on this Earth, most have a genuine attraction to the opposite sex. This attraction is systemically natural to them. There are others on this Earth, those in the minority, who have an attraction to the same sex or are equally attracted to both sexes. This attraction is also systemically natural to them. Without a doubt these forms of love exist. There is room on this Earth for those who wish to procreate, those who wish to share an intimate life with that of the opposite sex, and those who wish to share their lives with that of the same sex. Life will not come to a tragic end as many may believe due to the presence of different expressions of affection. There is not a conspiracy to convert the unwilling heterosexual community into a life of homosexuality. The labeling of right and wrong, natural or unnatural will never breed conformity. It will only perpetuate lies, and breed hatred, pain, violence and sometimes death.

For life to be created, a sperm and an egg is a required; hence male and female. That is a fact. What is also a fact is that love and partnership does not go hand in hand with procreation. Some may *want* it to go hand in hand but it doesn't necessarily *have* to. Reflect on the many children who have been unintentionally conceived. Now reflect on how many devoted couples wish not to procreate or have reach a point in their lives where they can no longer procreate. I can confidently say that most acts of consensual sex are performed out of lust and passion; not procreative intentions. People whether they are young, old, married, unmarried, gay, straight, infertile, or fertile can affectionately love each other without these creative intensions. Homosexuals do not wish to procreate together. We know the impossibility of that, to date. We wish to express a sense of intimacy and share our personal lives with the same gender. In saying we wish not to procreate with each other is not the same as wishing not to bear or adopt children. Some of us do wish to adopt and raise children. Some lesbians wish to bear their own children, and some gays wish to father their own rather than adopt.

The starting point for a clear understanding of natural and unnatural is the separation of love and procreation. With that as a given, now ask yourself truly what is "natural." Love is a visceral feeling **personal and natural** to an individual. Shame on the person who has the audacity to tell you how you feel or should feel.

What we have termed *love* is actually a somatic explosion mixed with emotional transduction intertwined in an all encompassing absolutism. Unfortunately, gays and lesbians are denied expression of this basic human phenomenon and are unnecessarily harassed because of what comes natural to us. We are deemed social deviants. Consequently, we resent and protest the injustice against us.

Change cannot come with complacency. The Human Rights war, for all parties concerned, comes with unavoidable fight, with unrest, with pain, with possible shame, and the spilling of innocent blood. The truth of pluralism and tolerance is right in front of all of us but, like a great conspiracy, it is masked by institutionalized hatred, misquoted scriptures, hypocritical belief in outdated laws, or phony science. The antagonists are never strong enough to admit their sins; sins of hate and blind ignorance. In their eyes the sins are upon the shoulders of the victims.

Many heterosexuals believe homosexuals should be mistreated. Many applaud, remain ambivalent, or, at the very least, turn a blind eye to the malice toward gays and lesbians. Statements I have heard are, "they bring it upon themselves", "they don't deserve any special treatment", "if they just stay quiet it would be fine", "they chose that lifestyle so it is their fault", "just stay away from me and my family", "as long as they do not rub their perversion in my face", "just keep it behind closed doors." There is no need for all of those nasty and isolatory rhetoric. We do not deserve that.

This is probably the most important yet most difficult concept to grasp. Sexual orientation is a persistent pattern of physical and emotional attraction or according to the American Psychological Association, "sexual orientation is an enduring emotional, romantic, sexual or affectional attraction to another person." [2] Attraction is the key word here. Someone can engage in sex without having an attraction, or they may enter into a marriage without having an attraction; they call it *act of convenience*. There are some people who live their entire life with an attraction only to that of the opposite sex or only to that of the same sex. Those, society calls heterosexuals or homosexuals respectively. There are those who have had an attraction to both sexes, although not necessarily at the same time. Those, society deemed as bisexuals.

Then, there are other important terms with which to become familiar. Gender identity is personal sense of maleness or femaleness. Most men feel like men, and most women feel like women with no reference to whom they wish to direct their intimate affection. Some biological men gender-identify with women and some biological women gender-identify with men. In other words, they feel like the opposite gender. Transgender is a label for those who live in the opposite society role of the physical sexual appearance. Most transgenders do not feel their biology is representative of who they are inside. Some rather than having surgery limit their expression of who they truly are by dressing, exhibiting mannerism, attitude, and physique of the opposite gender. Others seek medical intervention through surgery, psychiatric assistance and hormone therapy to correct the discrepancy. Usually the term transsexual is reserved for those who are post operative, but before surgery, some transgenders first undergo hormone therapy that transforms their body, besides the sex organs, to that of the opposite sex. If they are in the process of change, those individuals are also called transsexuals (pre-operative). So terms used are *pre or post trans-male* and/or *pre or post trans-female*. A trans-male is a person living as a man but was born female. A trans-female is a person living as a woman but born male.

Transvestitism is temporarily dressing in clothing and expressing the external style of opposite gender for pleasure. Transvestitism does not necessarily equate to homosexuality. Androgyny simply means having physical characteristics or mannerisms of both stereotypical male and female. Here is where the confusion comes into play for both the gay and straight community when trying to classify, categorize and group. I believe there is confusion because we are all unclear of what sex (being male/female) really is. Try this one on for size. A post-operative trans-male is having a relationship with a man. Technically this is a heterosexual relationship. Is it obvious what his male partner is? But, what about the trans-male himself? He has two x chromosomes, and on "his" birth certificate it reads female. Being female and attracted to a man is definition of heterosexual, but the previous "she" is now a man, living the life and in the biological body of a man, so is "he" gay? I guess what I am asking is, 'is sexual orientation based on original biological sex, unchangeable genes, present biological sex, or social gender?' Will society, fully aware of the situation, accept the union of these two men? Will society accept the union of a trans-female and a *"straight"* man just because it looks "normal"? Technically, the trans-female and straight man's union is a homosexual relationship based on genes or original biological sex.

Ok, now for an easier one. A post operative trans-male attempts to marry a woman. The groom is a self proclaimed heterosexual because "he" loves women, especially his wife to be. But is he really heterosexual and allowed to marry? After all he was born a girl. His wife-to-be identifies as a lesbian because she fell for him when he was pre-operative and looking like a woman. She still is very attracted to women, although devoted to her fiancé. Is she really a lesbian or now bisexual because of the actions of someone else? What makes a man a man and a woman a woman? Is it his or her sexual organs or gender identity? How will society judge two people looking like women at the alter (one a trans female and the other a non trans-female)? Technically these two can marry because the union, if based of genes, is heterosexual. In the proceeding chapters, to avoid the confusion, when referencing an attraction to a particular sex, I am referring to an attraction to the corresponding gender as well. In other words, when writing about a man and his love for a woman, I am referring to their biology and gender identity being one.

A person's sexual orientation is a fixed part of their biological and psychological make-up and cannot be chosen, changed, acquired, adopted or converted to. To say one has changed orientation is inaccurate; their bisexuality is just manifesting itself. To try and pigeon hole people into one category or another is defeating because there always exists that gray area. In referring to the gray area I mean that we will never know what is in the person's heart or what may lie in the future. When the social stigma becomes less severe or when the need to pursue happiness outweighs the negative stigma, the propensity will show itself more. It is nothing of which to be to be ashamed.

Homosexuality, as heterosexuality, is not just a behavior. It is a state of mind. Some homosexuals express their affection towards those of the same sex; some do not for several reasons. The ones that do not may believe that in expressing their homosexuality they will be damned to hell, so they live in a lie and chronic dissatisfaction. That lie, in itself, would damn them to hell anyway if you think about about. Some may fear being imprisoned, stoned, beaten, raped or worse. It does not change the fact that they are homosexual though. Turning the tables, being a heterosexual man or woman does not necessarily mean that one is presently having perverted or non perverted indiscriminant sex with women or men respectively. It means, if I am not mistaken, that they have an exclusive attraction, whether it is acted on or not, the opposite sex but not necessarily everyone of that sex. That, unfortunately, is not the standard society in general holds for gays and lesbians. There is a false assumption that we all are having sex with or want to make advances toward everyone (adult and child alike) of the same sex. That is wrong; very wrong.

According to the American Psychological Association:[2]

1) Human beings can not choose to be either gay or straight. Sexual orientation emerges for most people in early adolescence without any prior sexual experience. Although we can choose whether to act on our feelings, psychologists do not consider sexual orientation to be a conscious choice that can be voluntarily changed.

2) The reality is that homosexuality is not an illness. It does not require treatment and is not changeable

3) Psychologists, psychiatrists and other mental health professionals agree that homosexuality is not an illness, mental disorder or an emotional problem

4) Studies comparing groups of children raised by homosexual and by heterosexual parents find no developmental differences between the two groups of children in

four critical areas: their intelligence, psychological adjustment, social adjustment, and popularity with friends. It is also important to realize that a parent's sexual orientation does not dictate his or her children's.

We are an oppressed group of people; therefore we will fight for fair and equal treatment. We will not stay quiet and accept the injustice. As heterosexuals proclaim their sexuality on all fronts of society, we too refuse to stifle our affection toward each other (keeping it behind closed doors), then lie about it or conform to a heterosexual society. With that said, we should not have to live in fear that we will be harmed or humiliated by intolerant heterosexuals. Some heterosexuals demand for us to conform rather than them becoming tolerant because they believe how we are is wrong, is sinful, is evil, and that our actions are an abomination. In this book I will attempt to help dispel such negativity.

Many live amongst us that look different and believe in different Gods, politics, schooling, ways of life, etc, and yet they are either tolerated, accepted or merely viewed as someone dissimilar; not ugly, not bad. You have little to fear from us homosexuals. As a matter of fact, we have more to fear from you.

Hatred is a learned behavior. People are either taught to hate or are driven to hate by specific personal experiences. It is appalling when the lesson in hatred is based on hearsay, legal mandates, Holy words of a misguided clergy, or based on hasty opinions formed from selected media projections. You see, many have been conditioned by negative images and propaganda into believing homosexuals are an abomination, are perverts, are deviants, and are sick in the true sense of the word. For example, it is still an absolute insult to be called gay or assumed to be gay. People actively attempt to distance themselves from this category and attributed social status.

As mentioned previously, people cannot be converted into homosexuals as some may think. It is a part of one's constitution; whether this constitution is acted upon or not. To say that gay people are child molesters is as asinine as saying straight people are child molesters. Some may be, but most, by far, are not. To argue that *most* child molesters are gay or straight is a defeating battle because of inaccurate labeling and biases in data collection. "*Pedophiles and hebephils*, acting on their urges, molest children" is a far more accurate statement. But society wants so eagerly to cast blame on the homosexual; so eager to hate. Why is that? In chapter 3, I will address the facts about Homosexuality and Child Molestation.

Similar to the child molestation fallacy, to say all gays are evil is as asinine as saying all straights are evil, yet so many of the world atrocities were committed by those who lifestyles lend themselves to intimate partnerships with that of the opposite sex. Look, there are criminals, perverts and extremists of all sexual orientations in this world. Please do not condemn one group for those crimes.

Oh my dear reader, there are so many groups in history that have fallen victim to prejudice. Historically, negative images were cast on the Gentiles, the Moors, the Hutu, the Jews, the Zulus, the Serbs, the Native Americans, and the African Americans to mention a few. Please do not repeat history.

Privileged people seem to get swept up in the concept of differences equating to good and evil, right and wrong, blessed and cursed, clean and the unclean, the righteous and the unrighteous, the just and the unjust. Seemingly innocent inward disdain naturally evolves into the desires for "the different" to go away or to conform. It is a cowardly plot of establishing power, staying in a predictable comfort zone, and to create a false sense of importance. When they, the "different", do not go away or do not conform, the privileged organize in numbers and commence in isolating "the different", humiliating them, oppressing them, disrespecting them, denying them and ultimately killing them; killing their soul first, then their person. They use interpretive and subjective science, the media, and scriptures taken out of context; anything and everything to justify their hatred and actions. Then they brainwash the young so they too carry the baton of blind ignorance.

Millions of people have died because of differences, and insanely enough, millions of people have rationalized the killing of those who are different. Terms such as ethnic cleansing, genocide, holocaust, racial violence, anti-Semitism, gay bashing, and trail of tears should ring a solemn bell of reality. No good has ever come from hatred.

So it is the intension of this book to recondition such attitudes by reminding the reader of his/her history, by addressing most of the misconceptions of homosexuality, and by reflecting on rights you may take for granted and the damage that is being done by denying good people of their most basic rights—dignity.

References

1. Covey, S. (1989). *Seven Habits of Highly Effective People: Powerful Lessons in Personal Change*. New York: Simon and Schuster.

2. American Psychological Association. (2006). *Resolutions Related to Lesbians, Gay, and Bisexual Issues*. Washington DC; [On-line] URL: http://www.apa.org/pi/reslgbc.html

2

Prejudice 101

I would like to wipe the slate clean. Can you imagine a world where we love and respect people for their goodness, for their kindness, merit, character, their friendship and for their contribution; not to hate reject, banish, disrespect them based on who they love, what color their skin is, what divine being they choose to worship, or where they call home? I would like to think that most people have a kind soul. That soul, however, may have been mis-programmed and misguided.

If history has taught us anything, I hope that it is that bigotry is unequivocally wrong. Laws in modern and ancient history were enacted supporting the unequal treatment of several groups of people. We know now that they were unjust. Laws banning antidiscrimination are by shear logic supporting discrimination and supporting hatred. What a price we all are paying for that revelation today. One has to realize that the current federal law does not prohibit discrimination against gay people; sexual orientation discrimination remains perfectly legal.

Perfect example: Todd was hired as an executive assistant. He was well qualified and for two weeks had been exceeding expectations, a team player, punctual, productive, and respectful. Sarah, his co-worker jokingly said, "Todd your desk is so bare, why don't you have any pictures on your desk?" Todd initially shrugged off the question. He started though looking around and realized that almost everyone had a picture of their spouse, boyfriend / girlfriend and/or pet on their desk; so apparently having personal effect on one's desk was not against company policy. The next day Todd brought in a 4 x 6 inch framed picture of his lover Josh. When Todd's boss asked him if Josh was his brother, he answered no, his lover. That afternoon, Todd was fired. The reason was not that he failed to fulfill the expectations of his employment. It was because he was gay. He did not violate any of the company's policies on fraternization nor went outside the discreteness of personal effects in one's office. Todd cannot sue his employer because sexual orientation discrimination is not illegal.

You are probably thinking that Todd does not need a special law to fight unfair termination. But unfortunately he does. That is why in Employee Manuals you see, "Company X will not discriminate against race, color, gender, religion, political affiliation, or national origin." That statement needs to be in writing for employees to be safe from discrimination. Since the prohibition of discrimination based on sexual orientation is not in writing, gay employees are not safe and they are at the mercy of the employer. Would a woman tolerate termination because she is a woman? Would a person of color tolerate that? Would an Iraqi-American tolerate that? Would the Courts uphold such discrimination if it was any other minority group? My Goodness, the NAACP, EEOC and AMWA would have a field day. As you know the courts/legal system prevents such blatant discrimination. I hope you are familiar with the Federal Equal Opportunity Statement published by the Department of Labor.[1] It references the Civil Rights Act of 1964 Title VII. It also has amendments to include age and disability.

The Civil Rights Act of 1964 prohibits discrimination in housing, education, employment, public accommodations, and the receipt of federal funds on the basis of race, color, gender, national origin or religion.[1]

Few companies and educational institutions have amended this EOS statement to include sexual orientation, but most companies do not include sexual orientation. So if a qualified gay or lesbian is overlooked for a position or unfairly fired, the employer can legally say, "Yep, That's right and there is not a damn thing you can do about it. I do not approve of your lifestyle and I do not like your kind. Get out of here. Scram!" This type of discrimination is legal.

African Americans

At some point in history the unequal treatment of many groups of people was actually legal and condonable, as they still are today toward homosexuals. There are still people living amongst us who were adamant in their unadulterated hatred toward people of color back in the day. These racist not only had the church and scientific scholars encouraging them, they also had the Jim Crow laws backing them as well. It was the general consensus that that, "Negroes are inferior, they lack intelligence to vote or hold office. 'Dem niggers will never live in "my" neighborhood. They will not play with my children, or swim in the same pool as me or my family. Those blackies should not eat where I eat or sleep where I sleep. They are dirty, they smell, they are savages and thieves. A Spade will never work for or with me. Hell will freeze over before I work for one of *those* people. I hate black people."

Below are examples of Jim Crow laws enforced in the past 50 years, but no longer legal.[2]

ALABAMA

- Nurses. No person or corporation shall require any white female nurse to work in wards or rooms in hospitals, either public or private, in which Negro men are placed.

- Buses. All passenger stations in this state operated by any motor transportation company shall have separate waiting rooms or space and separate ticket windows for the white and colored races.

- Restaurants. It shall be unlawful to conduct a restaurant or other place for the serving of food in the city, at which white and colored people are served in the same room, unless such white and colored persons are effectually separated by a solid partition extending from the floor upward to a distance of seven feet or higher, and unless a separate entrance from the street is provided for each compartment.

FLORIDA

- Intermarriage. All marriages between a white person and a Negro, or between a white person and a person of Negro descent to the fourth generation inclusive, are hereby forever prohibited.

- Cohabitation. Any Negro man and white woman, or any white man and Negro woman, who are not married to each other, who shall habitually live in and occupy in the nighttime the same room shall each be punished by imprisonment not exceeding twelve (12) months, or by fine not exceeding five hundred ($500.00) dollars.

- Education. The schools for white children and the schools for Negro children shall be conducted separately.

GEORGIA

- Restaurants. All persons licensed to conduct a restaurant, shall serve either white people exclusively or colored people exclusively and shall not sell to the two races within the same room or serve the two races anywhere under the same license.

- The Board of Control shall see that proper and distinct apartments are arranged for said patients, so that in no case shall Negroes and white persons be together.

- It shall be unlawful for a white person to marry anyone except a white person. Any marriage in violation of this section shall be void.

- No colored barber shall serve as a barber [to] white women or girls.

- The officer in charge shall not bury, or allow to be buried, any colored persons upon ground set apart or used for the burial of white persons..

- All persons licensed to conduct a restaurant, shall serve either white people exclusively or colored people exclusively and shall not sell to the two races within the same room or serve the two races anywhere under the same license

LOUISIANA

- Housing. Any person ... who shall rent any part of any such building to a Negro person or a Negro family when such building is already in whole or in part in occupancy by a white person or white family, or vice versa when the building is in occupancy by a Negro person or Negro family, shall be guilty of a misdemeanor and on conviction thereof shall be punished by a fine of not less than twenty-five ($25.00) nor more than one hundred ($100.00) dollars or be imprisoned not less than 10, or more than 60 days, or both such fine and imprisonment in the discretion of the court.

NORTH CAROLINA

- Textbooks. Books shall not be interchangeable between the white and colored schools, but shall continue to be used by the race first using them.
- Libraries. The state librarian is directed to fit up and maintain a separate place for the use of the colored people who may come to the library for the purpose of reading books or periodicals.

VIRGINIA

- Theaters. Every person ... operating ... any public hall, theatre, opera house, motion picture show or any place of public entertainment or public assemblage which is attended by both white and colored persons, shall separate the white race and the colored race and shall set apart and designate ... certain seats therein to be occupied by white persons and a portion thereof, or certain seats therein, to be occupied by colored persons.

WYOMING

- Intermarriage. All marriages of white persons with Negroes, Mulattos, Mongolians, or Malaya hereafter contracted in the State of Wyoming are and shall be illegal and void.

The point here is, that which is legal may not be just, fair or "right."

Racists had, at the time, extremely convincing Christian and Judaic arguments to hate or minimize people of color and, there was little anyone could do or say (at the time) to change their minds. They pounded their fist to the Holy Bible stating that Abraham, Issac, Jacob and Job were slave owners. They quoted Leviticus 25: 44-46: "Your male and female slaves are to come from the nations around you; from them you may buy slaves. You may also buy some of the temporary residents living among you and members of their clans born in your country, and they will become your property. You can will them to your children as inherited property and can make them slaves for life, but you must not rule over your fellow Israelites ruthlessly." They also used the story of the Curse of Canaan to justify slavery and later discrimination against blacks. A Jehovah Witness publication is quoted, "The curse which Noah pronounced upon Canaan was the origin of the black race."[3] I feel the lazy amongst them that tried to use this Biblical reference did not really know the story to which they were basing their hatred. They just said, "It is the Bible that black people are to be slaves." Lets take a look at that scriptural story where that biblical justification from which it came. First, Ham, son of Noah, was labeled and assumed to be the father of the black race (although never referenced in the Bible as such). He, Ham, publicize the nakedness of his father, Noah, who outraged, cursed Ham's son Canaan to be the slave of his other sons.[4, 5]

According to Genesis 9:18–29,
18   Now the sons of Noah who came out of the ark were Shem and Ham and Japheth; and Ham was the father of Canaan.
19   These three were the sons of Noah, and from these the whole earth was populated.
20   Then Noah began farming and planted a vineyard.
21   He drank of the wine and became drunk, and uncovered himself inside his tent.
22   Ham, the father of Canaan, saw the nakedness of his father, and told his two brothers outside.
23   But Shem and Japheth took a garment and laid it upon both their shoulders and walked backward and covered the nakedness of their father; and their faces were turned away, so that they did not see their father's nakedness.
24   When Noah awoke from his wine, he knew what his youngest son had done to him.
25   So he said, "Cursed be Canaan; A servant of servants He shall be to his brothers."
26   He also said, "Blessed be the LORD, The God of Shem; And let Canaan be his servant.
27   "May God enlarge Japheth, And let him dwell in the tents of Shem; And let Canaan be his servant."
28   Noah lived three hundred and fifty years after the flood.
29   So all the days of Noah were nine hundred and fifty years, and he died.

The Curse on Canaan had nothing to do with the origin of the black race as some have contended. Ham had three sons besides Canaan. Cush was the father of the Ethiopians, Mizraim of the Egyptians, Phut of the Libyans and the peoples of Africa (see Genesis chapter 10). The curse placed on Canaan has to do only with Canaanites, a people who showed none of the racial characteristics of the black race according to historians and anthropologist. The problem concerning the Canaanites was not in the color of their skin but rather in the condition of their hearts. Yet this is the argument the Mormons, the white separatists, the anti-mongrelizationists, and those of the pre civil right era used to justify discrimination. That is scary. The story of Canaan is used also it condemn mixed marriage through these quote, Genesis 28:1, says that the Canaanites were the "servants of servants" and Isaac called Jacob and said unto him, "Thou shalt not take a wife of the daughters of Canaan." Those against mixed marriage are assuming again that the Canaanites were black. Biblical stories taken out of context can fuel a movement based on false information. These accounts then justified deprivation, persecution, and murder of millions of people. Later in chapter 4, I will address the scriptures that are used to condemn homosexuals.

Negative attitudes have stemmed from what was taught as history; historical "facts" most of us took as Gospel. Negative assumptions stemmed from what was portrayed in literature, in cinema, and in the visual arts. Scientists and science books brainwashed the young and the gullible. For example, a textbook published in 1914 by George W. Hunter titled *A Civic Biology*, was used for 3 decades in high school biology classes all over the Americas.[6] In the section on evolution under the subtitle 'The Races of Man', Hunter stated that,

"At the present time there exists upon the earth five races or varieties of man, each very different from the other in instinct, social customs, and to an extent, in structure." The five races were then ranked from inferior to superior as follows: "There are the Ethiopian or Negro type, originating in Africa; the Malay or brown race, from the islands of the Pacific; the American Indian; the Mongolian or yellow race, including the natives of China, Japan and the Eskimos; and finally, the highest type of all, the Caucasians, represented by the civilized white inhabitants of Europe and America."

The textbook stated that the 'highest' race is the Caucasians, who are specifically 'higher' developed in terms of 'instincts, social customs, and ... [physical] structure.

Also, typical of the views of the educated at that time was an article in the Encyclopedia Britannica which, under the heading 'Negro', stated[7]:

"By the nearly unanimous consent of anthropologists this type occupies ... the lowest position in the evolutionary scale ... the cranial sutures ... close much earlier in the Negro than in other races. To this premature ossification of the skull, preventing all further development of the brain, many pathologists have attributed the inherent mental inferiority of the blacks, an inferiority which is even more marked than their physical differences ... the development of the Negro and White proceeds on different lines ... in the former the growth of the brain is ... arrested by the premature closing of the cranial sutures ... The mental [differences] are at least as marked as the physical differences ... No full blooded Negro has ever been distinguished as a man of science, a poet, or an artist ..."

Science was wrong. The scientists were wrong. They led Americans to believe falsely and develop false "truths" of people of color. Beware of what the bigoted scientists' "claim" a homosexual is. In chapter 5, we will visit various theories and evolution of gay science.

Politicians, although holding public office, do not always fight for righteousness and fairness as some may think, but have their own agendas and wear their bigotry on their sleeves when they draft laws and implement policy. We must not look to them to be our moral conscience. Prejudice is wrong; plain and simple. Many common citizens are extremely impressionable and are influenced when they see and hear a popular political figure taking a stand for or against an issue. Case in point was Orval Faubus governor of Arkansas. He was the one that ordered the National Guard to stop black students from entering Central High School back in 1957. Then, when it was mandated by a Federal court order to let the students into the school, he did not reverse his orders to the National Guard. He rather intentionally and maliciously ordered all the Guardsmen to leave, leaving the students unprotected. Needless to say, absolute mayhem ensued.

Then there was George Wallace, governor of Alabama, who stood on the steps of the university denying entry to the newly enrolled black students, proudly proclaiming his pro-segregationist stance. Pro segregationists of the time used rhetoric to disguise their bigotry; using words like "separate but equal" yet fully aware that Black schools had suffered neglect. In South Carolina, Alabama and Mississippi, for example, white schools had flushing toilets, but Black schools had outhouses. Some Black schools had no running water or electricity; others lacked desks, gyms, libraries and auditoriums. Per-pupil spending in Southern Black schools was 45 percent of white schools and in Mississippi in particular, it was just 15 percent. Black teachers and students worked hard to compensate for the glaring inequalities, but Black Americans still suffered higher rates of illiteracy.[8] In the mist of all this inequality came the IQ tests, then the low scores were used as fuel for the argument of ignorance. Because one holds office does not make their decisions remotely admirable. Today, laws, and those who draft laws championing gay discrimination, are literally condoning discrimination. It is just as equally ignorance driven.

Jews

The persecution of Jews can be traced as far back as 2nd century BCE through writings and oral history. Antiochus attacked Jerusalem and called Judaism "inimical to humanity". Copies of the Torah was confiscated and burned, and an altar to Zeus erected. In 38 CE there was the first recorded mob attack against the Jews. In that year in Alexandria (Egypt), Flacuus, the Roman governor, ordered the attack on thousands of Jews. In 132 CE, Judea, the Jewish state, was wiped off the map and re-named Palestine, a Muslim state, and the Jews were forced out of their own country. Laws were enacted in the 4th, 5th, and 6th century forbidding Jews to socialize with Christians or to own slaves (common in those times). In Europe, Russia, and the Arab countries in the later 6th century, Jews were forbidden to hold office and employ Christian servants. During the Crusades, a series of Papacy sanctioned military campaigns, soldiers went to war to take Jerusalem from the Muslims. Those accompanying the first three Crusades though attacked Jewish communities in the mist, and put to death thousands of Jews in England, France, and Germany. In the Middle-Ages, in the mist of the Black Plague the Jews were falsely accused of poisoning the drinking water and falsely accused of murdering Christian babies in ritual sacrifice. Many as a result were lynched, brutally slaughtered, and driven out of several European countries.[9]

People have hated the Jews for centuries claiming they are subhuman, obtrusive, cunning, greedy, the killer of Jesus Christ, and that they lack social tact. The reputation of Jews being "greedy money lenders" stems from the Middle Ages where in those times it was illegal for Christians to lend money. Money lending, seen as a 'devilish trade', was one of the only professions allowed to Jews, who were forbidden to engage in most other economic activity. This increasingly led to the stereotyping of Jews as 'greedy moneylenders' seeking to ruin Christians. When economies were stressed, Jews would be the first to be blamed by the authorities who found them to be useful scapegoats during times of crisis.[10]

For two thousand years, the Jews have been blamed for the death of Jesus Christ (a Jew himself), which has been one of the root causes for anti-Semitism all over the world. But in early Christian texts it clearly outlines the Romans as his executioner. Scholars believed that the writers of the gospel revised the story in order to appease the Roman Empire and secure the longevity of Christianity in the empire. The clear disparity between the two gospels is evident. It wasn't until 1967 when the Vatican finally validated and admitted the fact that the Jews did not crucify Jesus.[11] Never the less, this early Biblical revision put into motion 2 millennia of anti Jewish antagonism.

Anti Semitism has left a despicable scar in modern and ancient history, but I am going to leap forward to one of the most poignant anti Semitic acts in modern history, the Holocaust. The Holocaust is a name applied to the state lead systemic persecution and genocide of the Jews, Romas (Gypsies), Poles, Serbs, Russians, mentally ill, homosexuals, Jehovah Witness, Communists, and political dissents of Europe and North Africa. They were deemed racially inferior and / or undesirables. The Jews made up 5–11 million of the victims although common figures use six million as their estimates. In addition to the Jews, 220,000 Romas, 2 million Polish gentiles, 700,000 Serbs, 100,000 Communists, 300,000 people with disabilities, 60,000 homosexual men and 2,000 Jehovah witnesses were killed. The Jews, by far, make up the majority of the victims of Nazi exterminations, but we must never invalidate the suffering of the other groups involved.[12]

Before the Final Solution, anti Semitism was rampant but not explosive in Europe. Adolf Hilter wrote a book titled *Mein Kampf* in 1925 laying out his anti-Semitism beliefs. It was virtually ignored though when it was first printed but then became a bestseller in Germany when Hitler gained political power in 1933. Before the actual systematic killing started, a series of events preceded in Germany, which is a sobering reality of how far written words and vocalized hatred can go. In 1933 after his book made the bestseller list, there was an organized boycott of all Jewish owned business. Then the Law of Restoration was passed. Under that law, Jewish civil servants in various city municipal levels of government were immediately fired. Then the Nuremberg Laws of 1935 stripped all Jews of German citizenship and of their basic civil rights and to vote. In 1936 Jews were banned from professional jobs exerting any influence in education, industry, and politics. In 1938 Jewish children were banned from attending normal schools. As the war started so did the massacres of Jews. That same year 1938 in one night, most of German synagogues were destroyed.[12]

As tragic as the Holocaust was, an equal travesty was international complacency. Are you aware that 31 countries, including the U.S. refused to accept Jews trying to escape Nazi Germany in 1938? In 1939 the Congress of the United States rejected the Wagner-Rogers Bill, an effort to admit 20,000 Jewish refugee children under the age of 14 from Nazi Germany.[13] In 1942, the details of the Final Solution were drawn up and carried out where the Jewish population were deported from the ghettos and all occupied territories; most sent to the extermination camps of Auschwitz, Chelmnom, Blezec, Treblinka among others. What started as an unsuccessful book culminated into 16 million deaths.[12] The reason cited was *ethnic cleansing*. It was not until June of 1944 that U.S finally allowed Jewish refugees from Italy to come to the States; 1,000 of them.[13]

Asians

Asian Americans and Pacific Islanders make up 9 million in the U.S. population, constituting 3% of the population. They make up 65% of the world's population. The majority of Asian Americans are college educated and with middle or upper income occupations. According to statistics, an Asian American is one and a half times more likely to have a bachelor's degree than a white non Latino and has an estimated 30% higher income than whites. Asian Americans include the Chinese, Japanese, Filipino, Vietnamese, Koreans, Indonesians, Thai and South Asians (Indians, Pakistanis, Sri Lankan, Nepalese, and Burmese).[14] Today, Asian Americans suffer from Hollywood style stereotypes as cunning savages, and prostitutes. Being smart investors and placing high priority in saving money, earned Asian Americans an ugly reputation of being ruthless cut-throat business people. Disgracefully, during the Rodney King riots in LA in 1992, 200 Asian American, but more specifically Korean, businesses were targeted, burned and looted. Incidentally, none of the acquitted police officers in the alleged assault of Rodney King were Asians and only one of the 12 jurors was Asian. Yet, Korean stores located in low income neighborhoods were targeted. Blacks in the neighborhood were resentful that the Koreans supposedly never hired Blacks to work for them, that they over charged, and that Koreans were parasites who exploited the community without giving anything back. When the anger ignited, the Koreans were victims of misdirected anger to institutional racism.

Some American institutions of higher education like Harvard, Brown, Princeton, Yale, and Stanford have restrictive admission policies for Asian Americans because too many Asians American students would over shadow the white college students. As of 2006, Asian students constitute 20% of the population at Ivy League schools. Having restrictive policy they have a habit of under admitting Asian student especially those with the highest academic test scores. There are no national organizations representing the interests of Asian Americans.[15, 16]

Before 1941 Asian American contributed tremendously to the developing of the West. They provided cheap labor on the nations railways and fed the American gold rush frenzy. They brought with them a rich history, intellect, and diversified all of the arts of the Americas, culinary, visual, literary, and the performing arts.[16]

Despite their contributions, an outrageous event took place in 1942 against innocent Japanese immigrants and first second and third generation Japanese-American. Due to racial hatred, fear and cruel stupidity, 120,000 of those American citizens and residents were assembled and forcibly relocated to concentration camps. Franklin Roosevelt himself authorized the rounding up through

Executive Order 9066. The event I am referring to was called **The Japanese American Internment**. Anyone with as little as one-eighth Japanese blood was sent to one of ten camps in Arkansas, California, Utah, Arizona, Wyoming, and Idaho.[17, 18] It wasn't until Feb. 1982 that a commission established by Congress issued a report entitled *Personal Justice Denied*, condemning the internment as "unjust and motivated by racism rather than real military necessity".[19] The Supreme Court ruled the interment illegal and unconstitutional. No formal apology was rendered until Sept. 1992 when George H. Bush issued formal apology from the U.S. government.

During the interment, most people lost everything they owned including their homes and businesses, and ultimately they lost their dignity. The conditions of the camps were deplorable. The cramped barracks were without plumbing or cooking facilities of any kind. There were also un-partitioned toilets, cots for beds, no privacy for married couples, and a budget of 45 cents daily per capita for food.[17, 18]

You see, after the attack on Pearl Harbor on December 7, 1941 by the Japanese empire, civilians and military officials had concerns about the loyalty of the ethnic Japanese on the West Coast and considered them to be a security risk, although these concerns often grew more out of racial hatred than actual risk. The underlying reason was using the war to justify and act upon their deep rooted contempt and disregard for the humanity of non-Anglos.

Internment was extremely popular among many white farmers who resented the Japanese American farmers. Below is a quote from the *Saturday Evening Post* in 1942:[19]

"We're charged with wanting to get rid of the Japs for selfish reasons. We do. It's a question of whether the white man lives on the Pacific Coast or the brown men ... If all the Japs were removed tomorrow, we'd never miss them in two weeks, because the white farmers can take over and produce everything the Jap grows. And we don't want them back when the war ends, either."

After lives were absolutely destroyed, the U.S government and the American people came back with, "Oops we were wrong," "So sorry". Ironically, considering his later position on civil liberty, Edgar Hoover was one of the few people in Washington against Executive Order 9066. Look, hatred-driven prejudice, isolation and civil deprivation are wrong. Hindsight is too late.

Women

According to Greek Methodology, Pandora, a woman, opened the forbidden box and unleashed plagues and unhappiness to mankind.[20] According to Genesis of the Bible, Eve, tempting Adam with the forbidden fruit, was the defining and unarguable cause of everlasting sin. Women also according to the Bible are endowed with the spirit of obedience.[21]

Genesis 3: 13-17
13. And the LORD God said unto the woman, "What is this that thou hast done?" And the woman said, "The serpent beguiled me, and I did eat."
14. And the LORD God said unto the serpent, "Because thou hast done this, thou art cursed above all cattle, and above every beast of the field; upon thy belly shalt thou go, and dust shalt thou eat all the days of thy life:"
15. "And I will put enmity between thee and the woman, and between thy seed and her seed; it shall bruise thy head, and thou shalt bruise his heel."
16. Unto the woman he said, "I will greatly multiply thy sorrow and thy conception; in sorrow thou shalt bring forth children; and thy desire shall be to thy husband, and he shall rule over thee."
17. And unto Adam he said, "Because thou hast hearkened unto the voice of thy wife, and hast eaten of the tree, of which I commanded thee, saying, Thou shalt not eat of it: cursed is the ground for thy sake; in sorrow shalt thou eat of it all the days of thy life;"

The natural biological role of women has traditionally been regarded as the social role as well. Females make up 51 % of the population in the U.S. as of 2006. In the middle of the 20th century they comprised 50% and at the turn of the 20th century they made up 51% of the population.[22] Despite their comparable numbers, males have monopolized the social economic and political strata. Women had to endure hundreds of years of oppression and we only pulled our plight to the forefront by becoming militant and "un-lady like. We did not wait for Congress, out of the goodness of their hearts, to grant us our due rights. We did not keep quiet and polite. We became publicly defiant to conventionality.

To deny women basic human right, the right of every human being, the sexists used biblical reasoning, biological reasoning, pseudo-legal reasoning and moral reasoning. Words like distasteful and sinful were used to describe the actions of women protesting and those who filed lawsuits. Words like unfit, unable, and inapt were used to deny inclusion. Comments like "they should know their place" were frequently uttered. "They should be seen and not heard". "Damn trouble makers". In shouldering the fight for equal rights many women became victims of slander, verbal and physical attacks, rejection, professional ruin, loss of livelihood and children. Remember though that before the black movement of the 1950 and 1960 black women even after the 1910 protests, were still denied basic rights so the uprising of the 1913–1919 was primarily a white woman's fight.

In just the past 100 years, the U.S. Congress, State governments, the majority of men, and some conservative women themselves were vehemently against granting women the right the vote, the right to work, equal wages, the right to enter into legal contract and the right to hold public office. If not legally enforced, there was certainly an undercurrent of discrimination in the workplace, in property and business ownership, in finance management to mention a few. Popular thought was that the woman's place should be in the home raising God fearing children, supporting her husband or the men in her life. After all, God intended it to be that way, right? But we now see it as oppressive now don't we?

Similar to state by state granting of gay and lesbian couples rights in custody, marriage and adoption cases, granting women the right to vote started too on state by state bases. Then and now suffrage (the right to vote), was determined by individual states not federally. In 1869 Wyoming became the first state to allow women to vote followed by Colorado and Utah. But in order to establish consistency across the union, an amendment needed to be made. In 1913 thousands of women paraded in Washington DC to raise awareness. The parade became violent with more than 100 women injured. The amendment failed several times in either the house or the senate before it finally was ratified in 1920.[23] Imagine the convincing arguments posed on the floor of the legislative branch of government to deny women. Now imagine the arguments today targeting gays and lesbians. As in the early 1900's, government today is blinded by their ignorance and power, and fearful to change practices not common or unpopular; although it may lift an oppressive situation.

Slowly and arduously, women fought for equal recognition and their equal place in society. It was not an easy road. We are living in a time where history is repeating itself. We gays and lesbians after years of oppression are taking our fight to the streets, to the media, to Congress, and fighting for what is fair. Evidence show we make good parents, yet we are denied adoption rights.[24] Evidence show we are less likely to molest children yet we are forcefully and publicly removed from teaching positions. FBI reports show as a group we are targeted by intolerant citizens more so than several groups included in the hate and bullying crime laws, yet we are excluded.[25] We are upholding the foundations and responsibilities of committed lifelong, loving, respectful, relationships, yet we are denied the right to marry. We are no more a public nuisance than straight people, yet we are denied access to certain public venue or if there is a small show of public affection we are asked to leave. Reflectively, "distasteful to see" used now with us as we become more visible was used with women when they strayed from the expected repressive norm behaviors into opportunities enjoyed by men. You see, "distasteful" has been proven over and over again as not a valid reason for oppressive laws. It seems to me that the problem lies, as proven over and over again, with insularity and hate. Why do we march? We march to bring awareness to the institutionalized hatred and the blatant partiality of the present laws.

Native American

Native Americans were victims of a philosophy called the Manifest Destiny in which the white European invaders saw themselves as having Divine right to take possession of all land and its fruits. Oh my Lord, where to begin with this group. After the arrival of Christopher Columbus, land was stolen from the Native American Nation. Men, women, and children were kidnapped, raped, and enslaved. Men, women, and children were slaughtered due the Europeans greed for land, power, and the spread of Christianity. Life sustaining crops and centuries of historical treasures were maliciously destroyed. Europeans brought to the Americas diseases like small pox, typhus, measles and influenza that wiped out 110 million Native Americans. They made and systematically broke peace and land treaties.[26] This was a wicked time in history. Congressman James M. Cavanaugh of Montana, in a debate on the floor of the House of Representatives in 1868, is remembered to have said: "I have never in my life seen a good Indian (and I have seen thousands) except when I have seen a dead Indian."[27]

The Europeans persistently encroached on tribal land driving the Indians off by force. In 1830, the Indian Removal Act was passed and by decree of the U.S Government. A hundred thousand Native Americans were forced to relocated from east of the Mississippi to west of the Mississippi. The Cherokee, Choctow, Creek, Chickasaw, and Seminole nations were led on a 1000 mile march to Oklahoma. More than 4,000 Cherokee died on what called the Trail of Tears but also over 5,000 Choctows, Creek and Chickasaw died on the march.[26, 28] Government claimed that the Native Americans were acquiring the vices of whites and claimed, altruistically, they were being removing their own good. The truth has well been established that it was the land and control that the government wanted. Following the removal there were many more wicked acts committed against Native American.

Due to European expansion into the Western territories soldiers, settlers and Indians often clashed. Although there was carnage on both sides, Native Americans noncombatant fatalities far outnumbered white. The bottom line was that White families and military brigades, with their armory, poor manners, ethnocentrism, and disease wanted land that had been hunted and lived on by those who were already there. Soldiers butchered 300 Suak and Fox men, women, and children at the Battle of Bad Axe in 1832 as they attempted to surrender. In 1864, 160 Cheyenne men women and children were massacred at Sand Creek, Colorado. Similarly at Wounded Knee, South Dakota in1890, 300 Sioux were killed and in 1863 200 Shoshones at Bear River Idaho to mention a few. Later that century, with only approximately 250,000 Native Americans left in United States, all reminding were move and confined to reservations, and had to adapt to austere life. They were allotted land that homesteaders and private interests did not want or could not use. The land was not ideal for cultivation yet they were restricted to a life of agriculture and not hunting. Stipends of goods and access to health care was promised but many times not delivered. Starvation was ramped and infant mortality rate was 5 times as high as the U. S. average. Despite deplorable conditions resilient families remained close and tried to preserve their traditional culture.

If it couldn't get worst, Native American children from the reservations between the ages of six and sixteen were forced to attend boarding school intentionally far away from the reservation. In accordance with U.S. government policy, attendance was mandatory. Families who resisted were severely punished and their limited rations on the reservation were cut-off. Justification at the time was based on the premise that "Indians had no written language and their children were unschooled. If these people, these Natives, were ever going to amount to anything in this United States of America, they had to be taught the proper and acceptable way to live." The policy was to "kill the Indian, save the man".[29] The children were to have absolutely no contact with family during their stay there at the school and in most cases were not allowed to go home during the summer months. Parents were forbidden to visit. They were given new names, forbidden to speak their native tongue, taught Christianity, and forbidden to practice tribal religions. School uniforms looking like military dress was required to be worn and tribal clothing was not permitted. At the Carlisle Indian School commencement, the superintendent Reverend A. J. Lippincott said. "Let all that is Indian within you die! ... You cannot become truly American citizens, industrious, intelligent, cultured, civilized until the INDIAN within you is DEAD."[29]

Mandated off-reservation boarding schools for Native Americans children continued well into the 20th century, finally closing the last school in 1933. The shameful outcome of these schools was cultural genocide.

Most are not aware that Native Americans were "granted" citizenship in 1924. Before then they could not vote, hold office, travel with a US passport, obtain federal government job etc. They were barred from Naturalization. Actually it was not until 1978 that The Indian Child Welfare Act ended discrimination that prevented Native Americas from acting as a foster parents or qualifying for adoption.

That same year The American Indian Religion Freedom Act was passes finally reversing U. S. policy outlawing tribal rituals and shamanic practices.

Are we any different today, given the opportunity to inflict suffering on an unprotected group of people? Are we any at all more sensible? The future will judge you on your actions today. Think hard on your attitudes.

We look back at those extreme times and most of us now say, "How awful a time it must have been, and how wrong a time that was." Yet it does not change the fact that it did take place and that line in the sand was drawn by those who were deemed intelligent people. Many suffered and many died. Many are still living with the physical and emotional scars of those times. "How could we allow such discrimination and injustice?" but aren't we living the history of our future? We *will* reflect on the human rights position we take today. I guarantee most misguided homo-hatists (homophobes) will say, "How could we have allowed such blatant discrimination?" "What the hell were we thinking?" "We should have known better." "How could we have been so blinded by the hysteria?" "I am so sorry for what I did, the many I hurt, and the stance I took." "Please forgive me."

I am not arguing that discrimination against Blacks, Jews, Asians, Women, Native Americans and homosexual precisely fall into the same category, or comparing one experience as the proportionally similar to another. The groups mentioned above have centuries of oppression, banishment, and slavery, and the numbers slaughtered are multifold over homosexuals. I am merely trying to illustrate that pseudo-science, the Bible beaters, society, and law makers are now setting their sites on the homosexual. Oppression is oppression no matter the degree, and we are fighting against it.

Please do not think, "Oh how extreme, how dramatic. That was then. This is now, and now is different." Believe me when I say, we are re-living history, right here-right now. How much more extreme can one get when two lesbians holding hands in public are brutally and publicly raped. This and many cases were not adequately investigated by the homophobic detectives, the assailants claimed sex was consensual and the credibility of the victims shredded when asked about their sinful, perverted and abominable lifestyle. The defendants, charged with assault and rape, were judged by their homophobic peers. They walked away from the court room as "innocent" free men. This is common in cases that actually reach trial where open homosexuals are victimized. Attitudes are that we brought it upon ourselves. What crime was committed here that "straights" do not themselves commit everyday in every town; holding hands? "They were lesbians, and people don't like lesbians, right? They should not hold hands—inappropriate social behavior. So, they should be tortured and humiliated. Homosexuals are evil, are perverts, and are sick in the true sense of the word evil." Or a young man is kidnapped, beaten, mutilated, and tied to a fence with an inch of his life because he was gay. As he laid in a coma, a University of Colorado fraternity paraded on a float through Ft. Collins, Colorado where he was hospitalized with a scarecrow tied to a fence. A sign on the scarecrow read, "I am Gay" This man, Matthew Shepard, later died of his injuries.[30] His murder was unprovoked. It could have been any gay man. "People do not like gays, so they should be tortured and killed. Homosexuals are evil, are perverts, and are sick in the true sense of the word." What crime was committed by the Jews to deserve extermination? "They were not Christians. They killed Christ. They poisoned the drinking wells. They were merely born. People do not like non Christian, murdering terrorists, so Jews deserve to die." What crimes did Blacks commit to deserve kidnapping, murder, enslavement, and lastly, but still today, oppression and deprivation? "They were not Anglos, they are subhuman, they are ignorant. People do not like subhuman, non-Anglo, dummies so they deserve what they got." What crime was committed by Asians-Americans to deserve interments and humiliation? "They were not Anglos, they are the enemies, they are whores, and railroad beggars. People do not like difference, and a good Jap is a dead Jap, so they deserve what they got." Oh, my dear reader, see the pattern? Prejudice and discrimination is wrong; plain and simple.

The fact is that gays are denied expression. If their sexual orientation is visible and/or verbally expressed they may be denied employment, residence, right to adopt, rejection from family, right to keep their own child, right to inheritance, right to marry, right to eat at a restaurant, right to be buried with family, right to register at a hotel, right to worship, right to the university of choice, right to their own safety, just to mention a few. Just imagine a world of heterosexual denial? Every aspect of socialization would come to a screeching halt. I am not just referring to sex but all aspects of human connection. That is what is asked from us. Some in the gay community, yes, are extremists and flaunt what most view as personal. But so do heterosexuals; in so many ways. There are extremists in your group too. My Lord, just turn on the TV, listen to the radio, go to the beach, or go to the club. Better yet, look in the front seat of a parked Lexus after the executive company party. Straights have all their business all out there for the world to see. Heterosexual themes are everywhere and intensions are certainly not kept behind closed doors. Yet, two gay men who lovingly gaze into each other eyes at a restaurant are asked to leave because they are "upsetting the customers". "Eww.. I do not need to see that!!"

A photo on a desk, an introduction, an embrace, a touch, a dance, and a gentle soft kiss are subtle forms of expression of affection. Straights do it, yet some become so intolerant when we do it. Later in Chapter 8, I will outline the specific civil liberties and social privileges that straights may take for granted and how gays are deprived of those basic privileges as citizen. As any vulnerable group, there should be laws or law inclusions to protect us. If there weren't crimes against us, we would not need to ask for protection.

I am gay. So what? Leave me alone, that's what! Do not hurt me. Don't take my children from me. Don't fire me. Don't conspire to get me evicted. Allow me to teach school if I so desire or hold office based on the common interest of my constituents. Don't kill me. Allow me to marry the consenting adult I love. Judge me on my character. Stop staring at me with disgust. Seat my lover and me at a restaurant. Do not ask my partner and me to leave the dance floor. Allow me to pay my respects and say goodbye to my partner on her dieing bed. Allow her to make medical decisions when I am incapacitated. Gives her the damn money I left her. Stop allowing the kids to beat up my sweet little girl because she has two Moms. And for God sakes, there is no need to avoid me. Why do we march? We march so we can live.

References

1. U.S. Department of Labor. (2006). *Federal Equal Employment Opportunity (EO) Laws*. Washington, DC [On-line] URL: http://www.eeoc.gov/abouteeo/overview_laws.html

2. Freman, D. (2000). *The Jim Crow Laws and Racism in American History.* Berkeley Heights: Enslow Publishers.

3. Watters, R. (1988, July/Aug) Blacks and the Watchtower. *Bethel Ministries Newsletter.*

4. Ham, K., & Wieland, C. (1999). *One Blood: The Biblical Answer to Racism.* Green Forest: Master Books.

5. Haynes, S. (2002). *Noah's Curse: The Biblical Justification of American Slavery.* Oxford: Oxford University Press.

6. Hunter, G. (1914). *A Civic Biology: Presented in Problems.* American Book Company.

7. *Encyclopedia Britannica,* 9th ed. (American Reprint), 1884, Vol. 17, p. 318.

8. Bollinger, M. (2004). "Brown v. Board: 50 years Later" *Socialist Worker,* p 8 May 14.

9. Timeline of Jewish History. [On-line] URL: www.wikipedia.com.

10. Poliakov, L. & Howard, R. (2003). *The History of Anti-Semitism.* Philadelphia: University of Pennsylvania Press.

11. Barrack, M. (2001). From Memory to Reconciliation. *The Catholic Faith.* Jan-Feb issue.

12. Bauer, Y. & Keren, N. (2002). *A History of the Holocaust.* Danbury: Franklin Watts.

13. Wyman, D. (1984). *The Abandonment Of The Jews: America and the Holocaust.* New York: Pantheon Books.

14. U. S. Department of Commerce. (2005). *Asian and Pacific Islanders in the United States. 2005 Census of Population.* Washington D.C.

15. Kitano, H. & R. Daniels. (1995). *Asian Americans: Evolving Minorities.* Englewood Cliffs: Prentice-Hall.

16. Daniels, R. & Kitano, H. (1970). *American Racism: Exploration of the Nature of Prejudice.* Englewood Cliffs, NJ: Prentice-Hall.

17 Burton, J. F., Farrell, M., Lord, F., & Lord, R. (2002). *Confinement and Ethnicity: An Overview of World War II Japanese American Relocation Site.* Seattle: University of Washington Press.

18. Masaru, B. (2004). *Democratizing the Enemy: The Japanese American Internment.* Princeton: Princeton University Press.

19. Report of the Commission on Wartime Relocation and Internment of Civilians. (1982). *Personal Justice Denied.* Washington DC: Government Printing Office.

20. Graf, F (1993). *Greek Mythology: An Introduction*. Baltimore: Johns Hopkins University Press.

21. "Genesis Chapter 3 Verses 13-17." *in The Holy Bible: 1611 Edition, King James version* [On-line] URL: www.biblegateway.com

22. National Population Estimates. [On-line] URL: http://www.census.gov/popest/national/asrh/NC-EST2005-sa.html

23. Scott, A. F., & Scott, A. M. (1982). *One Half the People: The Fight for Woman Suffrage*. Philadelphia: Illini Books.

24. American Psychological Association. (2004). *APA Policy Statement: Sexual Orientation, Parents and Children*. Washington DC. [On-line] URL: http://www.apa.org/pi/lgbc/policy/parents.html

25. Federal Bureau of Investigations. (2005). *Hate Crime Statistics 2004*. U.S. Department of Justice. Washington DC. [On-line] URL: www.fbi.gov/ucr/hc2004/openpage.htm

26. Perdue, T. (1988). Trail of Tears. In P. Weeks (Ed.), *1524—The Present: The American Indian Experience (*pp 96-117). Arlington Heights: Forum Press.

27. Burton S. (1948). *The Home Book of Proverbs, Maxims, and Famous Phrases*. New York: Macmillan.

28. Fleming, Walter. (2003). *The Complete Idiot's Guide to Native American History*. Alpha Books: New York.

29. Colman, M. (1993). *American Indian Children at Schools 1850–1930*. Jackson: University Press of Mississippi.

30. Gross, L. (2004). *Up from Invisibility*. New York: Columbia University Press.

3

Child Molestation

Most would agree that the sexual abuse of children is a despicable and iniquitous act. Those who commit such crimes against children are wicked and monstrous predators. We all want to protect the vulnerable in our communities; the young, the old, the infirmed; those who cannot fight for themselves but blaming gays in general for child molestation is just wrong. American singer and political activist Anita Bryant who successfully campaigned in the 1970s to have gay discrimination re-established was quoted in saying, "a particular deviant minded [gay] teacher could sexually molest children."[1] "If gays are granted rights, next we'll have to give rights to prostitutes and to people who sleep with St Bernard's and to nail biters."[1]

According to the Bureau of Justice Statistics,[2] the facts are as such. Female children are six times as likely as male children to be victims of sexual assaults. More specifically, 86% of all victims of child sexual assaults are females. Nearly all of the offenders in sexual assaults reported to law enforcement were male (96%). Fifty percent of sexually abused boys and twenty percent of sexually abused girls are victimized by juveniles, with the mean age of the molesters at 14 years old.[3]

In most cases, the sexual orientation of the offender is not investigated, it is assumed that when a man assaults a girl, he is heterosexual or if the man assaults a boy he is homosexual. It is that assumption is inaccurate. Most adult child molesters have surrounded themselves with a lifestyle that draws little attention. In other words, heterosexual themes like wife or girlfriend, children, and stable job. It has also been reported that most child molesters are not fulfilled in their relationships with adults. Ninety-six percent of men who have been arrested or who sought treatment for molesting a boy or boys report having no desire of being with men or have ever had a relationship with men. Ninety—two percent of men who have been arrested or who sought treatment for molesting a girl or girls express not being fulfilled with sexual relationships with women, and wish not to be with men. Twenty-one percent of pedophiles who were charged with molestation of girls reported that they also molested boys and fifty three percent of those charged with molesting boys reported they also molest girls. It is suffice to say that age is driving force, not gender, in pedophilic behavior.[4]

Let me digress a bit though and define various terms for you. **Pedophilia and hebephilia** are diagnostic terms. Pedophilia is an adult psychosexual disorder characterized by a preference for prepubescent children as sexual partners. Hebephilia is adult sexual attraction to adolescents or children who have reached puberty. Not all pedophiles and hebephiles actually molest children; an adult can be attracted to or would prefer to have sex with a child or an adolescent over an adult without ever actually engaging in sexual contact with them. **Child molestation and child sexual abuse** are terms used to describe actual sexual contact between an adult and someone who has not reached the legal age of consent and sexual molestation is used to describe non consensual sexual contact with other.[5]

Canadian researcher, Bogaert, and associates showed that homosexual males responded no more to male children than heterosexual males respond to female children.[6] Penis volume was monitored as subjects were inundated with nude visual images and audio sexual equivalent of children. Please note that many adults may be attracted to children but they do not prefer children over relationships with adults nor would they act on their attraction toward children. Speaking of which did you see the 2006 Victoria Secret show? The models were dressed as little baby girls carrying bottles and pacifiers. Apparently the producers and organizers of the show felt a need to cater to the pedophilic nature of their mostly heterosexual male viewers. Was that supposed to sexy or sick? Other adults have absolutely no physical attraction toward children and would find such thoughts and/or actions revolting.

In analyzing correlation between sexual orientation and child molestation, Dr. Carole Jenny reviewed 352 medical charts representing all the sexually abuse children seen in emergency rooms and child abuse clinics of a Denver children hospital during a one year period. Where an adult molester could be identified (269 of the 352 cases), their adult sexual orientation was investigated. The molester was a gay or lesbian adult in only 2 of the 269 cases.[7] In other words, those living a homosexual adult lifestyle, according to this localized study, are not likely to be the offender of such crimes yet it still stands that those living a homosexual adult lifestyle or those who are un-closeted homosexuals are frequently subject of suspicion for sexual abuse and child molestation. Why is that?

As mentioned above, most male to male child molesters surround themselves with adult heterosexual themes and most have never been involved nor desire to be intimately involved with an adult male. So are these criminals homosexual, heterosexual, pedophiles or combination there of? They do not like men so technically they are not gay (homosexuals). But, they are attracted to boys. Hmm? But outside of preying on children, they live heterosexual lives. So are they straight (heterosexuals)? Confusing? It doesn't have to be. Ask yourself, "How would you label a man who molests a girl and returns home to a male lover?" Most of you are probably answering "GAY!" Ok, now ask yourself, "How would you label a man who molests a boy and returns home to a wife or girlfriend? "Most of you are still saying, GAY!" That's how the media characterizes him. Now why is that, when he doesn't desire men? On what are they basing this call? Is it on who they molest or their adult sex partners? The answer is really very simple. The criminal is a pedophilic male to female or male to male child molester who may *project* a particular adult lifestyle. Their lifestyle is a more accurate criterion on who they are, straight or gay. If their lifestyle is questionable, then assumptions **cannot be made**. They are simply, "child molesters with *undetermined* sexual orientation;" not automatically GAY!! There are far more male to female child molestation cases and convictions yet those criminals are not labeled "straight" and then the entire group (heteros) deemed unsuitable to be contact with children. They are viewed as they should, as pedophiles. By sheer statistics and numbers openly gay adults are less likely to molest children. The automatic assumption that male to male child molesters were homosexuals, and then the entire community put in suspect was the major flaw in Paul Cameron's article; an article often used by right wingers against gays.

Paul Cameron is a very well known individual in the antigay community who wrote one of many explosive articles. One was titled, "Child Molestation and Homosexuality" and was published in 1986 in Psychological Report[8]. Although published in 1986, from the turn of that decade he was making claims that homosexuals were mass murders and child molesters and citing other researchers for those findings.[9] Since then, he has been quoted countless of times by antigay organizations, politicians, and church leaders in their attempts to link homosexuality with child sexual abuses. Unfortunately, the gullible public and religious congregations latched on to his statement, "Studies have been done that prove homosexuals are child molesters".[8] His article supports the answer 'Yes' to the question, 'Do those who commit homosexual acts disproportionately incorporate children into their sexual practices?' His article claims that at least one third of the sexual attacks upon youths are homosexual (male to male) and that those who are bi or homosexual are proportionately much more apt to molest youth than are heterosexuals.

Instead of using crime reports from state law enforcement agencies, department of justice documents, or FBI data bases, he left surveys on door steps. Having a 23% return on his 550 question survey, his respondents, according to sociologist, were likely those who would exaggerate their sexual experience to poke fun of such an invasive survey. Back in the 1980's high-quality surveys typically obtained response rates around 75% or more.[10, 11] Assumptions were also made that male to male sexual assaults were committed by adult homosexuals without consideration of the actual orientation of the assailant or taking into consideration cross gender abuses. He totally twisted other researchers' studies to favor his claims. According to Dr. Natalie Porter at the University of Nebraska, "If you read their research, they have in no way made such claims. We have letters from those researchers saying his work has distorted their research."[12]

The methodological flaws in his study have since been revealed, and his pseudoscientific statements since been discredited by the American Psychological Association (APA).[13] As a matter of fact, the APA disassociated themselves from Paul Cameron and his claims. On December 2, 1983, the American Psychological Association sent Paul Cameron a letter informing him that he had been dropped from membership.[14]

"This is to notify you that the Board of Directors of the American Psychological Association on December 2, 1983 voted to drop you from membership in the Association for lack of cooperation with the Committee on Scientific and Professional Ethics and Conduct; this is a violation of the preamble to the Ethical Principles of Psychologist. Consistent with Article II Section 19 of the Bylaws, you may re-apply for membership after five years has elapse. Yours Truly, Max Siegel PhD President"[14]

In the winter of 1984, all members of the American Psychological Association received official written notice that "Paul Cameron was dropped from membership for a violation of the Preamble to the Ethical Principles of Psychologists" by the APA Board of Directors.[13] At its membership meeting in October, 1984, the Nebraska Psychological Association adopted a resolution stating that it "formally disassociates itself from the representations and interpretations of scientific literature offered by Dr. Paul Cameron in his writings and public statements on sexuality."[15] In 1985, the American Sociological Association (ASA) adopted a resolution which asserted that "Dr. Paul Cameron has consistently misinterpreted and misrepresented sociological research on sexuality, homosexuality, and lesbianism" and noted that "Dr. Paul Cameron has repeatedly campaigned for the abrogation of the civil rights of lesbians and gay men, substantiating his call on the basis of his distorted interpretation of this research."[13]

Back in the 1980's Cameron cited a 1978 study by Groth and Birnbaum[16] that evidenced 3:2 ratio of female victim to male victim molestation. Cameron took that information, and assumed that all male to male molestation was committed by homosexual males and that *not* all the male to female molestations were committed by heterosexuals; the *bisexual correction* he called it. He then stacked the "3" of that ratio with this bisexual correction. Only he, not the Groth / Birnbaum study, concluded that 54% of all molestations were hence performed by bisexual or homosexual practitioners.[8] Once again, he cited Groth and Birnbaum's 1978 study, but Groth and Birnman's study reported none of the men in their sample had a homosexual adult sexual orientation and none of the 22 bisexual men were more attracted to adult male than adult females.

In another article published in 1985,[17] Cameron claims that a student is about 90% times more likely to be sexually assaulted by a homosexual teacher. This was based on 30 instances of sexual contact between teacher and pupil. The ratio rose to100% times more likely when Cameron added his *bisexual correction.* Scientifically and ethically, this ratio is meaningless because no data were obtained concerning the actual sexual orientation of the teachers involved. Additionally questionable surveys were used to gather information. Once again, he assumed that male—male contact were perpetuated by homosexuals. This was the infamous argument used for years to vilify homosexual educators, scout leaders, and potential adoptive parents. The damage is far reaching because so many people have now been programmed to think we are molesters based on indirect knowledge of Cameron's claims.

Empirical research does not show that gay or bisexual men are any more likely than heterosexual men to molest children. This is not to say that homosexual and bisexual men never molest children, as it would be inaccurate to argue that heterosexual men never molest children. But there is no scientific basis for asserting that homosexuals are more likely than heterosexual men to do so. At this point I would like to quote the same Dr. Nicholas Groth[18] whose legitimate research was misrepresented by Paul Cameron.

"Are homosexuals adults, in general, sexually attracted to children and are preadolescent children at great risk of molestation from homosexual adults that from heterosexual adults? There is no reason to believe so. The research to date all points to there being no significant relationship between a homosexual lifestyle and child molestation. There appears to be practically no reportage of sexual molestation of girls by lesbian adults and the adult male who sexually molest young boys is not likely to be homosexual."[18]

Dr. Groth complained to the Nebraska Board of Examiners of Psychologist that Cameron,

"… misrepresents my findings and distorts them to advance his homophobic views. I make a very clear distinction in my writing between pedophilia and homosexuality, noting that adult males who sexually victimize young boys are either pedophilic or heterosexual, and that in my research I have not found homosexual men turning away from adult partners to children." "I consider this totally unprofessional behavior on the part of Dr. Cameron and I want to bring this to your attention. He disgraces his profession."[19]

When it is all said and done, is it assumed that heterosexual men indiscriminately lust after little girls or that heterosexual women prey on little boys? They, after all, are attracted the opposite sex. So why is it assumed, without substantiated evidence, that homosexual men molest little boys or that lesbians violate little girls?

Is it assumed that heterosexuals, in general, will sexually harass their opposite sex subordinates in the workplace, and not likely to exercise good judgment and appropriate discretion? So why is it assumed, without substantiate evidence otherwise, that homosexuals will aggressively pursue those of same sex? Why is it assumed that we are less capable of controlling our sexual urges?

We face these stigmas everyday when filing custody and adoption papers, while around young family members, applying for jobs involving children, helping with field trips and car pools, coaching, and running for public offices. Handed that challis of tainted water, people drank hardily. Now they hate us and so they demonize us. Please accept this cup of truth. We are not criminals.

References

1. Bryant, A. (1977). *The Anita Bryant Story: The Survival of our Nations families and the threat of militant homosexuals.* Old Tappen: Fleming H. Revell.

2. Synder, H. (2000). *Sexual Assault of Young Children as Reported to Law Enforcement: Victim, Incident and Offender Characteristics.* U.S. Department of Justice. Bureau of Justice Statistics, National Crime Victimization Survey, Washington, D.C.

3. Ryan G, Miyoshi T.J., Metzner J.L. (1996). Trends in a national sample of sexually abusive youths. *J. AM. ACAD. Child Adolesc. Psychiatry,* 35 (1), 17-25.

4. Abel, G. N. Harlow (2001). *The Stop Child Molestation Book.* Philadelphia: Xlibris Corporation.

5. America Psychological Association (1987). *Diagnostic and Statistical Manual of Mental Disorders* (3rd ed., Revised) Washington DC: Author.

6. Bogaert, A. F. & Hershberger, S. (1999). The Relation Between Sexual Orientation and Penile Size. *Arch Sex Behav,* 28 (3), 213-21.

7. Jenny, C., Roesler, T.A. & K.L. Poyer. (1994). Are Children at Risk for Sexual Abuse by Homosexuals? *Pediatric,* 94 (19), 41-44.

8. Cameron, P et al. (1986). Child Molestation and Homosexuality. *Psychological Reports,* 58, 327-337.

9. [On-line] URL: http://www.qrd.org/qrd/religion/anti/cameron/background.and.rebuttal

10. Intelligence Report. (2005). *Garage in Garbage Out: Paul Cameron Discredited Research remains a Mainstay of the Antigay Rights.* [On-line] URL: www.splcenter.org

11. Herek, G. M. (1991). Myths about sexual orientation: A lawyer's guide to social science research. *Law & Sexuality,* 1, 133-172.

12. David R. (1985, August 20). Gays Assail Dennemeyer for Hiring Researcher. *LA Times Metro.*

13. [On-line] URL: http://psychology.ucdavis.edu/rainbow/html/facts_cameron_sheet.html

14. Seigal, M. (1983, December 2). *APA letter by Max Seigel to Paul Cameron.* [On-line] URL: http://psychology.ucdavis.edu/rainbow/html/Cameron_apaletter.html

15. Nebraska Psychological Association. (1984, October 19). *Resolution. Minutes of the Nebraska Psychological Association.* Omaha, Nebraska: Author.

16. Groth, A. N., & Birnbaum, H. J. (1978). Adult Sexual Orientation and Attraction to Underage Persons. *Archives of Sexual Behavior,* 7 (3), 175-181.

17. Cameron, P. et. al. (1985). 'Homosexual Molestation of Children/Sexual Interaction of Teacher and Pupil.' *Psychological Reports,* 57, 1227-1236.

18. Groth, A. N., & Gary, T. S. (1982). Heterosexuality, homosexuality, and pedophilia: Sexual offenses against children and adult sexual orientation. In A.M. Scacco (Ed.), *Male rape: A casebook of sexual aggressions* (pp. 143-152). New York: AMS Press.

19. Nebraska Board of Examiners of Psychologist. (1984, August 21). *Letter written by Dr. A. Nicholas Groth.* [On-line] URL: http://www.qrd.org/qrd/religion/anti/cameron/background.and.rebuttal

4

The Scriptures

The Bible holds much reverence in the Christian and Jewish communities. The Holy Bible (for the most part) is packed with stories of love, peace, tolerance, and respect. It is one of the most powerful books known to humankind and still is a bestseller today. But for those who promote an agenda of hatred and greed, the Holy Scriptures can be easily misinterpreted and misused. It is important then to ascertain the context of any verse before making sweeping generalizations about them.

Let's say your verse identifies a person based on his or her crime (i.e. deceit) against God or "man". It then describes the "rightly deserved" punishment received from the heavens, and for some reason the verse also identifies the person as a homosexual. Do not interpret and generalize all homosexuals as such criminals. That is not intelligent. It would be as inaccurate to label all heterosexuals as Judas-es. He was, as far as we know, a heterosexual. So since a straight guy betrayed Jesus, should therefore all straights be betrayers? Better still should all heteros hang themselves from the nearest tree? See how ridiculously silly an interpretation that would be?

In this chapter I will discuss the most controversial of the scriptures; the scriptures the Christian Conservatives use to justify their hatred, and support their condemnation of gays. These are Genesis 1: Creation of Adam and Eve, Genesis 19: The Story of Sodom and Gomorrah, Leviticus: the Mosaic Code, Romans 1: same sex behavior as reprehensible, and 1 Corinthians: The clobbler passages.

Before I start quoting the Bible, I would like to address two schools of thought for those Christians who hold the Bible scared. Liberal and conservative Christians interpret the Bible differently which unavoidably leads to two contradictory sets of beliefs on many topics (raising of children, shaving, eating of pork, farming, role of women in society, virgin marriages, divorce, worshiping, etc). Homosexuality is, of course, no exception.

Generally speaking, the conservative Christian believes that the Bible was written by authors who were directly inspired by God. The writings in the Bible are inherently free of error. The Bible is the actual Word of God. Generally, the liberal Christian believes that the Bible was written in the pre-scientific age which treated slavery, genocide, mass murder and the oppression of women as acceptable. They clearly understand the flaws and concentrate on the applicable messages of life. When liberal Christian readers study the Bible for guidance on homosexuality, they generally look for applicable Biblical themes, like those advocating justice, love, monogamy, caring, commitment, etc.

We can no longer use the term *The* Bible, but rather *A* Bible. Are you aware of how many versions or translations of the Bible there are? There are over a hundred versions just in English.[1] There is even a misleading one called the Dead Sea Scroll version, but be aware that it is a translation that was created in 1999 not the unadulterated long lost Dead Sea Scrolls.[2] Now, I give credit where credit is due. The New American Standard Bible, for example, was translated over a period of 10 years, by over 45 scholars and was first published in 1962. Similar painstaking work was applied to the production of the New International Bible of 1978, the King James of 1611 and the New King James of 1982.[3] These translations and others like them were the products of many years of work from scholars from many denominations. Some, if not most passages, have remained unchanged throughout time, but others have changed in the story line, semantics and therefore in meaning. This happened either to conveniently suit a given agenda or in hopes of delivering a moral message **the theologians not God** found fitting at the time.

The more the Bible is re-written into "modern language" the more the Bible is defused of its original meaning or taken out of context. For example the word homosexual is now freely used in the Bible. The term was coined in 1869 in German and 1892 in English, not when the original Bible was written.[4] So if this and other modern words had been incorrectly inserted due to misinterpretation by theologians, it was then scripted in *the* bible as *the* Word of God" and believed by millions over the years as *the* word of God. Those are not God's word, those are words of man; one that may have been filled with bigotry or ignorance at the time. Case in point is the term "effeminate". Below are the same verses from different version of the same book of the Bible.

> **King James Bible:** <u>1 Corinthians 6:9-10</u> "Know ye not that the unrighteous shall not inherit the kingdom of God? Be not deceived: neither fornicators, nor idolaters, nor adulterers, **nor effeminate**, nor abusers of themselves with mankind, Nor thieves, nor covetous, nor drunkards, nor revilers, nor extortioners, shall inherit the kingdom of God."[5]
>
> **The Amplified Bible:** <u>1 Corinthians 6:9-10</u> "Do you not know that the unrighteous and the wrongdoers will not inherit or have any share in the kingdom

of God? Do not be deceived (misled): neither the impure and immoral, nor idolaters, nor adulterers, nor those who participate in homosexuality, Nor cheats (swindlers and thieves), nor greedy graspers, nor drunkards, nor foulmouthed revilers and slanderers, nor extortioners and robbers will inherit or have any share in the kingdom of God."[6]

Today, most definitions for "effeminate" are based on culturally defined criteria, such as clothing styles, hair length, or mannerisms, such as a high-pitched voice, limp wrists, or an upper class accent. That was not the case of the early Bibles. Matter of fact, effeminate or effeminati was a word inserted in Corinthians in the 4th century.

The oldest known Bible version to mankind is the Masoretic Text. It was a compilation of the Dead Sea Scrolls and confirmed as early as 168 BC. The Masoretic Text was written entirely in Hebrew, and this text became the standard authorized Hebrew Bible around 100 AD. The Leningrad Codex is the oldest surviving complete copy of the Masoretic text. It is dated at 1008 AD and has been housed at the Russian State Library since 1863. The Old Testament of the Bible existed prior to the writing of the New Testament and, unlike The Old Testament, The New Testament was written in Greek rather than Hebrew. The earliest available New Testament is the Greek Koine Bible of 56AD. The Greek and Hebrew Bibles were translated into Latin in the 4th century, and in 1524 the world saw the first printed English translation of the Latin Bibles.[3]

When examining the original meaning and context of 1st Corinthians one needs to seek out the earliest New Testament version of that canon, which is the Greek Kione Bible. In 1: Corinthians 6:9, "effeminate" is not scripted. First of all, effeminate is not a Greek word nor does it have Greek origins. It is a word rooted in Latin. In 1st Corinthians, the Greek word used was Malakos, which literally means soft, but it also carries connotations of moral laxity and weakness, cowardliness, vainness in appearance and jewels.[7, 8] In ancient cultures for a man to shave would be considered Malakoised.[8] In other cultures, a man who boastfully wore fine flashy clothes would be considered the same. "Malokoi" was used in the Greek Koine Bible of 56AD and seen in the 1624 Elzevir edition used today.[7] "Effeminati", as the Latin translation, crept into the Jerome's Vulgate in 382AD and then "weaklings" in the English Bishop's Bible in 1568.

1: Corin 6:9-10. Knowe ye not that the unrighteous shall not inherite the kingdome of God? Be not deceived: neither fornicatours, nor idolatours, nor adulterers, nor weaklinges, nor abusers of them selves with mankinde, Nor theeves, nor covetous, nor drunckardes, nor cursed speakers, nor pyllers, shall inherite the kingdome of God[9]

In The King James Bible 1611 (original), in place of weaklinges, "effeminate" appeared:

1 Cori 6: 9-10. Know yee not that the unrighteous shall not inherite the kingdome of God? Be not deceived: neither fornicatours, nor idolaters, nor adulterers, **nor effeminate**, nor abusers of themselves with mankinde. Nor thieves, nor covetous, nor drunkards, nor revilers, nor extortioners, shall inherit the kingdom of God.[10]

In the American Standard Bible of 1901 we see "effeminate" still scripted:

1 Corin 6: 9-10. Or know ye not that the unrighteous shall not inherit the kingdom of God? Be not deceived: neither fornicators, nor idolaters, nor adulterers, **nor effeminate**, nor abusers of themselves with men, nor thieves, nor covetous, nor drunkards, nor revilers, nor extortioners, shall inherit the kingdom of God.[11]

Suddenly, in 1958, the Amplified Version instead of "effeminate," it is written "those who practice in homosexuality".[6] The New English Bible of 1961, "homosexual perversion," crept into the verse.[12] In the Today's English Version of 1963, they followed suit and wrote "homosexual perverts", and the New American Catholic Bible of 1970 also has, "homosexual perverts." The Living Bible of 1971 has "homosexuals", the New International version of 1973 has homosexual offenders, the New King James version of 1979 has "homosexual," the New Living Bible of 1996 has "male prostitutes", and the Holman Christian Standard Bible of 1999 has both "homosexuals" **and** "male prostitutes".[13, 14, 15, 16, 17, 18, 19] How did *Malakos* get so twisted?

The story of Sodom and Gomorrah (Genesis 19) is an interesting one; with one dramatic discrepancy due to mistranslation. As the story goes, the Lord and two angels were on their way to Sodom and Gomorrah when they visited with Abraham who was camping near a town called Mamre. He told Abraham that they were on their way to the city (Sodom) to first confirm that wicked people and deeds were being committed and then to destroy the entire city. That did not sit well with Abraham and he asked the Lord if he would spare the city if 50 innocent people could be located. The Lord said yes. Abraham went further to asked if 45 could be found would he spare the city, and bartered even more with 30, 20, and finally 10. The Lord said "yes" he would spare the city if 10 could be found. The two angels traveling with the Lord went on their way to Sodom where they ran into a man by the name of Lot at the city gates who urged them to eat with him and spend the night at his home. Lot knew they were angels and addressed them as such. Initially saying no, the angels reconsidered and accepted the invite. This is where the story goes array.

In most English translations it reads that after Lot and the angels ate, all the men (young and old alike) of the city gathered in a mob like fashion outside Lot's home demanding that Lot send out his male guests so they can have sex with them. Other translations have that all the town people of the city gathering in a mob like fashion outside Lot's home demanding that Lot send out his guests so they can "know" them.

New International Version Genesis 19: 4-5:
4. Before they had gone to bed, all the men from every part of the city of Sodom—both young and old—surrounded the house.
5. They called to Lot, "Where are the men who came to you tonight? Bring them out to us so that we can have sex with them."[20]

King James Version Genesis 19: 4-5:
4. But before they lay down, the men of the city, even the men of Sodom, compassed the house round, both old and young, all the people from every quarter:
5. And they called unto Lot, and said unto him, "Where are the men which came in to thee this night? Bring them out unto us, that we may know them."[21]

Tanakh (Hebrew Bible) Bierthshi (Genesis) 19: 4-5:

4. טֶ רֶם שָׁ כָ֫ בוּ יְ שָׁ נֵ אַ וְ הָ עִ יר שֵׁ יר אַ נְ סָד׳ מִ י סַ נְ בּ וּ

מְ קָ צֶ,ה:ם כָּ ל־ הָ עָ ן וְ עַד־ זָ קֵ ן מְ בַּ יִת עַל־ הַ בַּ

5. יְ קָ רְ א וַ וַ אֵ ל ־ ל וֹט י׳   וַ אָ ֵ ֯ וּ לֹ אמְר וּ   הָ אֲ נָ שֶׁ ה

[22] אֶ שֶׁר־ בָּ   אֲ אֵ ל אוּ   הַ לֵ יךָ   הַ יְ לָ ה ה וֹ צִ יאֵ ם אֱלֶ ם   וְ נֵ דְ עָ ינוּ א תָ,ם:ה

Translation: Late evening, all mortals of Sodom stormed the home where the angels lodged. They called to Lot, "where are the guests lodging here tonight? Bring them out that we may know them."

The consensus among the many versions and translations of the Bible was that rape was the intent of the mob, but it is in the development of the attempted crime that they differ. As with the word *Malokoi*, I decided to research the true essence of the story through studying the Hebrew Bible and Hebrew transliterations. The Hebrew Bible, in identifying who stormed the house **and** who the mob asked Lot to release, was the word *eenowsh* (שׁ נ א ן י) or אנוּ שׁ which is pronounced en-oshe. The word means *mortal* or is a general term for non-gender specific *mankind*. In Hebrew, to identify a human as a man or that of the male gender is the word *iysh* (שׁ אִי) pronounced eesh is used, and to identify a woman the word *ishshah* שֶׁ הָ אִ שׁ נ שׁ ימָא pronounced is-shaw is used.[23] Again, in the Hebrew Bible concerning the story of Sodom and Gomorrah, the term *enowsh* שׁ נ א ן י ' was used, not *iysh*.[22]

The Hebrew Bible was the one that preceded the Latin, which preceded the English translation.[3] Furthermore, *Iysh,* **not** used in this story, was used in other stories as Numbers, Genesis, Ezekiel, Kings, 1 & 2 Samuel, Judges and Proverbs, where *Iysh* was used to identify men as specifically male.[24]

Unquestionably, it can be concluded that the towns people or the mortals (men and women) surrounded the house and demanded that Lot release his gender unidentified guests. The mob was still unaware of whether the visitors were male or female. Somewhere along the lines of translation the word *men* (maybe unintentionally) was inserted and *male* assumed.

To continue with the story, Lot refused to release his guests (angels) to the mob but tried to appease them by offering his virgin daughters. The mob refused and more forcefully demanded the guests be released to them. At that point the Lord intervened and blinded a few of them and, after commanding Lot (and family) to leave the city, then destroyed Sodom. When Lot offered his virgin daughters to the mob and they refused, the story makes sense because the daughters were certainly not the strangers. If Lot had young boys in his home and offered them, the mob too would have refused. The mob wanted the strangers, whatever gender they were. It was not about homosexual sex, it was about being inhospitable and nasty to strangers.

The sin of Sodom and Gomorrah was inhospitality, not homosexuality. Hospitality was a primary obligation for persons in ancient cultures, especially Israel.[25] The way that the people of Sodom treated the two angelic guests showed criminality, disrespect, and their lack of hospitality. Most of the biblical translations of Genesis 19 fail to acknowledge that it was the whole community—male & female, young & old—who came to Lot's house and demanded that Lot turn his guests over to them. When the reader realizes that it was not just a group of men who demanded to "know" the male visitors, then the possibility of seeing the story as being about homosexual behavior disappears.

Rape and non procreative sex in Christian and Jewish ancient societies has been look upon with disdain, and once State and religion became one in the Roman and Syrian Empires, sex of this sort became illegal. *Lewd* was the term given to this form of sex. One of the earliest surviving uses of the word *sodomite* was in a letter written by Burchard, Bishop of Worms, in the 2nd millennium advising his parish priests to ask about sodomy in confessionals. He advised them to ask, if the parishioner had committed rape, adultery, bestiality, fornication like that of a sodomite, and if women used devises for sexual pleasure. What was also asked was "have you inserted your rod (virga) in the rear (posteriora) of a male and in this way has intercourse with him like a sodomite."[26] This last sentence is what was held on to for years to come. All of the sexual acts mentioned, rape, adultery, bestiality, etc, were that of a "sodomite" not just rear penetration. But, as with the biblical interpretations, lewd acts became sodomy, and eventually anal sex (heterosexual and homosexual) in particular started to be used interchangeably with sodomy. Law texts and legislation into the 20th century used the term freely strictly referring to anal sex. It is no wonder the Bible changed its interpretation in the middle of the 1900s. In the 1970 *sodomy* became the general term for gay sex not just anal sex, and it took until 2003 for the Supreme Court to strike down Texas Sodomy law banning private consensual sex between adults of the same sex. This ruling invalidated similar laws through the U.S. It is way too late to turn back the hands of time.[27]

Sodomy and *sodomite* are so ingrained in our consciousness because that is the only term we know for anal penetration. I take issue the negative evolution of the term. Preachers and lawmakers lash out against us, calling us such names and their naïve supporters internalize such hateful attacks. Inhospitality and an overall sinful existence caused the destruction of Sodom. Homosexuals were not to be blamed.

As the Dhammapada is to the Buddhist, the Bhagavad Gita to the Hindu, and the Qur'an is to Islam, the Bible is a very powerful book for both Jews and Christians. It is a collection of 66 individual books divided into two main sections: the Old Testament containing 39 books and the New Testament containing 27 books. Archeological evidence through tombs, excavation sites, scrolls and inscriptions have validated the names of many people, places and certain historical events in both the New and Old Testament. The original books of the Bible were authored by leaders of tribes, people hailed as prophets, and followers of Jesus Christ.[3] The stories serve to reveal God, instill principles of ethical conduct, answer life's great questions, and to direct the steps of mankind. As mentioned above, it was, though, written in the pre scientific era by mortal men. Now, it is debatable if these men were truly inspired by our loving and forgiving God, or rather inspired by the time, social climate, political ambitions, and their own experiences.

The questions of, 'where did I come from?' 'where am I going?', 'how should I act?' 'why is this happening', 'what should I expect from myself and others,' 'who will protect me,' 'who is judging me' have plagued us for thousands of years. To live a fulfilling life or a life with some sense of predictability, we seek the answers to these questions. Once found or thought to be found, we hold on to those answers as if we are holding on to our very existence. Structure lessens chaos. It is difficult to grasp that occurrences may happen by shear chance, or that we may be alone, or we may never be forgiven. That will leave us vulnerable; without any control over our destiny. Humans cannot work in those conditions, so we reach out to the external for answers.

Biblical stories developed and were written to give rhyme and reason to life. Hope can be a good thing; so we do not give up trying, but *blind* faith is a thinly veiled argument to justify ignorance. Blind faith is the unwillingness to question and a suspension of rational thought. There is irrefutable evidence that the universe came into existence 14 billion years ago[28, 29] yet with Genesis dating the creation of the world, moon, sun, and stars at 4004 BCE many still hold firm to that belief. Furthermore, even if you do not subscribe to the complete theory of evolution, it is truly bind faith to intelligently believe that humans were created out of dust.[30, 31]

The stories of the Bible have profound spiritual meaning and there are countless lessons to be learned through them. The stories of the Old and New Testament, though, were written and intended for ancient Hebrews and Greeks, and many of these stories cannot be applied to the era we live in today. To single out the story that fuels your hatred and disregard the rest is hypocritical.

In antiquity, towns and villages were under constant attack. Mortality rates were high and age of mortality was low. In those times, it would be beneficial for couples to have many children. Today the earth is over populated and over polluted. There are corrupt governments depriving citizens' access to food, water, and shelter. In order to maintain a certain standard of living, millions of people are doing all they can, legal and illegal, to limit the amount of children they have. The all-time most popular quote of Genesis, "Be Fruitful and Multiply"[32] is no longer wise. Given the earth's overpopulation, it is detrimental to the future of human existence to be fruitful and multiply. The story of Adam and Eve was a story of the two essential entities for life to come forth and multiply. It is not a story of love, commitment, truth, respect, and partnership. God created Adam. He blessed him, created a woman Eve from one of his ribs, and commanded them to multiply in numbers, and to fill the earth and subdue it. He commended them to rule over the fish, birds and every living creature, and also to not eat form the tree of knowledge of good and evil or they would surely die.

Believe me, there will never be *that* many homosexuals to reverse the growth rate of the world. The world will continue in it's out of control spiral to self destruction without any help from us. When people scream, "God created Adam and Eve not Adam and Steve." I agree with them; geniuses. If you take the Bible literally then yes, for babies and population growth, it was necessary for a male and female to be originally created. Doh, Sherlock!!

The Bible was written in an era where respectable sexual activity was between men and women who were wed until death for the main purpose of procreation and economics.[33] Although polygamy was acceptable, lust, fornication (premarital sex), divorce, and intimacy with a divorce woman was not acceptable.[34, 35, 36, 37] Unnatural sex according to the Bible include anyone engaging in sex for pure enjoyment, unmarried couples engaging in sex, and married couples engaging in sex where one or both may be infertile. So straight out of the starting blocks, there are many amongst us, if not most, that should be condemned, right? No, we just live in a different time now.

The Third Book of Moses is called Leviticus. It is this book that outline's God's law to the Israelites. Moses is said to have written Leviticus at the foot of Mount Sinai. The two passages below from the King James Version is what the homo-haters use against homosexuality.[38, 39]

Leviticus 18:22   Thou shalt not lie with mankind, as with womankind: it is abomination

Leviticus 20:13   If a man also lie with mankind, as he lieth with a woman, both of them have committed an abomination: they shall surely be put to death; their blood shall be upon them.

Both seem very clear cut, but equally as clear and beyond refute are the rest of the Holiness codes. It just so happens that the clergy has deemed the other codes obsolete and have focused on those passages concerned with homosexuality. Why is that?

Leviticus 11:1-8   Say to the Israelites: 'Of all the animals that live on land, these are the ones you may eat: You may eat any animal that has a split hoof completely divided and that chews the cud. There are some that only chew the cud or only have a split hoof, but you must not eat them. The camel, though it chews the cud, does not have a split hoof; it is ceremonially unclean for you. The coney, though it chews the cud, does not have a split hoof; it is unclean for you. The rabbit, though it chews the cud, does not have a split hoof; it is unclean for you. **And the pig,** though it has a split hoof completely divided, does not chew the cud; it is unclean for you. You must not eat their meat or touch their carcasses; they are unclean for you.[40]

Leviticus 11:9-11:   Of all the creatures living in the water of the seas and the streams, you may eat any that have fins and scales. But all creatures in the seas or streams that do not have fins and scales—whether among all the swarming things or among all the other living creatures in the water— you are to detest. And since you are to detest them, you must not eat their meat and you must detest their carcasses. Anything living in the water that does not have fins and scales is to be detestable to you.[40]

According to Leviticus 11, we shouldn't be munching-out on bacon, shrimp, or lobster, yet Christians who participate in such "detestable" behavior are not called to repent, nor is IHOP or Red Lobster picketed. On Christmas do we or do we not partake in the Christmas ham. Read your Bible, "And the pig … is unclean for you."

Leviticus 19:12   You shall not swear by my name falsely and profane the name of your God[41]

If someone uses the name of God vain, an indiscretion that goes against the Mosaic laws and the Ten Commandment, they are not held in contempt. Names include but not restricted to, "God Damn, Jesus, God, and Jesus Christ" Some Christians have even been tricked into using take-offs of the Lords name such as Geeze (short for Jesus), "Good Gosh," "Gosh Darn," and "Lordy." In certain circles, since these innocent phrases are actually take offs and intended to mask the Lord's name, one who curses with it, is still cursing God based on who and what they imply.

Leviticus 19: 9   When you reap the harvest of your land, you shall not wholly reap the corners of your field.[41]

In abiding with the Mosaic laws, how many farmers leave the corners of their field un-harvested? None I tell you. NONE!!

Leviticus 19:19   Do not breed any of your domestic animals with other of the same species do not sow a field of yours with two different kinds of seed and do not put on a garment woven with two different kinds of thread.[41]

It is common practice to crossbreed cattle sub species, swine, and fowl. The majority of American and European farmers should be labeled as sinners and treated as such, but they are not.

19:19 forbids sowing a field with mixed feed, yet farmers are not condemned who, as a common practice, plant both alfalfa and hay. So many people today wear blends of thread like polyester and cotton; forbidden in this same verse.

Leviticus 19:27   Do not clip your hair at the temples nor trim the edges of your beard[41]
Leviticus 19:27   Do not lacerate your bodies and do not tattoo yourself[41]

19:27 forbids shaving and tattoos yet men are not condemned if they are clean shaven. Both women and men sport tattoos today as fashion statement. Tattoo parlors, Gillette and Remington headquarters are not picketed or forced to close because of a state petition by right wingers or Christians conservatives. And how many of us have some sort of piercing. Hello!!

Leviticus 19:26   Do not eat meat with the blood still in it.[41]

19:26 forbids the eating rare, medium rare, and medium meat, yet a family has moral impunity upon leaving the local Outback Steakhouse after their prime rib dinner.

Leviticus 19:32   Stand up in the presence of the aged and show respect for the old.[41]

Leviticus 19:33   When an alien reside with you in your land do not molest him. You shall treat the alien who resides with you no differently than the native born among you.[41]

19:33 forbids treating immigrants (legal or otherwise) differently, yet the George W. Bush administration deprives employment and legal shelter to undocumented immigrants. As a matter of fact, sends them packing.

Leviticus 20:9   Any person who curseth his mother or father must be killed.[42]

20:9 forbids verbally lashing out at parents under penalty of death, yet it is tolerated, condoned and even glamorized on children's TV shows as the Simpson's.

Leviticus 20:10   If a man cheats on his wife or vise versa both the man and the woman must die.[42]

20:10 forbids infidelity yet it is an accepted indiscretion and it is glamorized on movies such as Bridges of Madison County and From Here to Eternity, and top TV drama shows such as Desperate Housewives; not to mention multiple soap operas watched by the same idiots who would vote for gay discrimination.

Leviticus 20:18   If a man lies in sexual intercourse with a woman during her menstrual period both of them shall be cut off from their people.[42]

Leviticus 20:27   A man or woman who acts as a medium or fortune teller shall be put to death by stoning. They have no one but themselves to blame for their death.[42]

20: 27 calls for the death of fortune tellers yet they are in multitude at fairs, in malls, on the boardwalk, and even at church carnivals. Fortune teller outfits and crystal balls are bought as costumes for little children to parade around their Christian neighborhoods asking for candy on the Day of the Dead no less (Halloween).

Leviticus 24:17   Whoever takes the life of any human being shall be put to death[43]

Contradictory, the sixth of the Ten Commandments reads, "Thou shall not kill",[45] Leviticus clearly instructs that if someone does so, they too must be killed,[44] yet we are still debating if capital punishment is just or not.

Leviticus 23: 3   Six days shall work be done: but the seventh day is the Sabbath of rest, an holy convocation; ye shall do no work therein: it is the Sabbath of the LORD in all your dwellings.[44]

According the Bible, the Sabbath is a day of rest, a day of no work, and day of no cooking fires.[44, 46]. The Sabbath humility includes not leaving home as well.[48] Moreover, the Bible points out that those who do not keep the Sabbath holy, must be put to death[49]. Keeping the Sabbath Holy is also the forth of the Ten Commandments. It is historically from sundown Friday to sundown Saturday although Christians have changed that Holy day to Sunday primarily because of when Jesus appeared in His resurrected form. Sunday is the new Sabbath for Christians.[50] I ask you, the reader, who stays home, under obligation, on Saturday and/or Sunday, or, besides daily chores,[51] does no work, does not cook, or does not light any fires?[52] Summer barbeques on the weekend is like an American tradition.

The irony is that most of the above scriptural quotes (including Leviticus 18 and 20) are actually moot or null void because, according to Acts 15,[53] Christians are not required to keep the Laws of Moses anyway.

The Book of Deuteronomy is the New Testament's Book of Obedience. Homo-haters also use this Book of the Bible to fuel hatred towards homosexuals (actually cross dressing), and justify our continuous condemnation:

The woman shall not wear that which pertaineth unto a man, neither shall a man put on a woman's garment: for all that do so are abomination unto the LORD thy God.[54]

As Leviticus, let's take a look at the some of my other favorite outdated biblical laws in Deuteronomy.

If thy brother, the son of thy mother, or thy son, or thy daughter, or the wife of thy bosom, or thy friend, which is as thine own soul, entice thee secretly, **saying, Let us go and serve other gods**, which thou hast not known, thou, nor thy fathers; Namely, of the gods of the people which are round about you, nigh unto thee, or far off from thee, from the one end of the earth even unto the other end of the earth; Thou shalt not consent unto him, nor hearken unto him; neither shall thine eye pity him, neither shalt thou spare, neither shalt thou conceal him: **But thou shalt surely kill him**; thine hand shall be first upon him to put him to death, and afterwards the hand of all the people.[55]
If a man have a stubborn and rebellious son, which will not obey the voice of his father, or the voice of his mother, and that, when they have chastened him, will not hearken unto

them: Then shall his father and his mother lay hold on him, and bring him out unto the elders of his city, and unto the gate of his place; And they shall say unto the elders of his city, **This our son is stubborn and rebellious**, he will not obey our voice; he is a glutton, and a drunkard. **And all the men of his city shall stone him with stones, that he die**: so shalt thou put evil away from among you; and all Israel shall hear, and fear.[56]

Let me conclude by quoting two more scriptures,

"He **without sin** among you, **cast the first** stone."[57]
'Teacher,' he said, 'which law is the greatest law of all?' Jesus said, ' "Love the Lord your God with all your heart. Love him with all your soul, and love him with all your mind." This is the first and greatest law. The second law of God is like it. "**Love your neighbour** as you love yourself."[58]

The stories of the Bible were written in a time and place different from what and where we live today, and they should not be held to absolute literal interpretation. It is written in the Bible that same sex male intimacy is an abomination, and that those who do not "keep" the Sabbath or those who try to convert another should be killed. As fire and brimstone have not destroyed the world due to the indiscretion of those who choose to light up that grill on Sunday or voice another belief, consenting men and women who choose to share an intimate life together will not force the world into chaos either. In other words, so what if a man wants to be with another man, or a woman with another woman? So what? So it looks funny. So what? A woman driving a car looked funny at one point and so did a black man in a polling station. So you don't feel the same way. So what? Don't date the same gender then. We have been brainwashed with selective condemnation. Relax. Do not fall victim to scriptural hypocrisy.

References

1. Rogerson, J. (2001). *The Oxford Illustrated History of The Bible.* New York: Oxford University.

2. Abegg, M. (1999). *The Dead Sea Scrolls Bible: The Oldest Known Bible Translated for the First Time into English.* New York: HarperCollins Publishers.

3. Friedman, R.E. (1989). *Who Wrote the Bible?* New York: Harper& Row, Inc.

4. Foucault, M. (1978). *The History of Sexuality. An Introduction, Volume One.* New York: Random House Inc.

5. "1st Corinthians Chapter 6: verses 9-10" *in The Holy Bible: 1611 Edition, King James version* [On-line] URL: www.biblegateway.com

6. "1st Corinthians Chapter 6 verses 9-10" in *The Holy Bible: 1987 Edition, Amplified version.* La Habra: The Lockman Foundation. [On-line] URL: www.biblegateway.com

7. "1st Corinthians Chapter 6 verses 9-10" in *The Holy Greek Bible: 1624 Elzier Edition,* Novum Testamentum Graece: Pierson Publishing Group.

8. Aland, K. (1966*). Greek New Testament with English Introduction including Greek/ English Dictionary.* United Bible Society

9. "1st Corinthians Chapter 6 verses 9-10" in *The Holy Bible: 1568 Edition, Bishop's Bible.* [On-line] URL: www.studylight.org

10. "1st Corinthians Chapter 6 verses 9-10" in *The Holy Bible: 1611 Edition, King James.* [On-line] URL: www.StudyLight.org

11. Schaff, P. ed. (2006). "1st Corinthians Chapter 6: verses 9-10" in *The Holy Bible: 1901 Edition, The American Standard.* New York: Thomas Nelson & Sons. [On-line] URL: www.biblegateway.com

12. Dodd, C.H ed. (1961). "1st Corinthians Chapter 6: verses 9-10" in *The Holy Bible: 1961 Edition, The New English Bible. New Testament.* Oxford and Cambridge: Oxford University Press and Cambridge University Press.

13. Olson R.A. ed. (1963). "1st Corinthians Chapter 6: verses 9-10" in *The Holy Bible: 1963 Edition New American Standard New Testament Today English Version.* La Habra: Lockman Foundation

14. Hartman, L.F., Bouke, M.M. eds. (1970). *The Holy Bible: 1970 Edition . New American Catholic Bible.* Paterson: St Anthony Guild Press.

15. Taylor, K.N. ed. (1971). "1st Corinthians Chapter 6: verses 9-10" *in The Holy Bible: 1971 Edition, The Living Bible Paraphrased.* Wheaton: Tyndale House Publishers.

16. Palmer, E.H. ed (1973). "1st Corinthians Chapter 6: verses 9-10" in *The Holy Bible: 1973 Edition. New International Version New Testament.* Grand Rapids: Zondervan.

17. Farstad, A. ed. (1979). "1st Corinthians Chapter 6: verses 9-10" in *The Holy Bible: 1979 Edition. New King James New Testament.* Nashville: Thomas Nelson.

18. "1st Corinthians Chapter 6 verses 9-10" in *The Holy Bible: 1996 Edition. The New Living Translation*. Wheaton: Tyndale House.

19. "1st Corinthians Chapter 6 verses 9-10" in *The Holy Bible: 1999 Edition. Holman Christian Standard*. Nashville: Holman Bible Publishers.

20. Palmer, E.H. ed. (1973). "Genesis Chapter 19: verses 4-5" in *The Holy Bible: 1973 Edition. New International Version New Testament*. Grand Rapids: Zondervan.

21. "Genesis Chapter 19 verses 4-5" in *The Holy Bible: 1611 Edition, King James*. [On-line] URL: www.biblegateway.com

22. "Bereshit Chapter 19 verses 4-5" in *The Hebrew Bible: 1008 Edition: Westminister Leningrad Codex*. [On-line] URL: www.sacred-texts.com

23. Doniach, N.S., and Kahane, A. (1996). *The Oxford English-Hebrew Dictionary*. New York: Oxford University Press Inc.

24. Brown, Driver, Briggs and Gesenius. "Hebrew Lexicon entry for 'iysh". "The Old Testament Hebrew Lexicon".
[On-line] URL: http://www.searchgodsword.org/lex/heb/view.cgi?number=376

25. Cook, E. J. (2006) "Hospitality Is Biblical—And it is Not Optional" in *This Rock*. El Cajon: Catholic Answers, Inc. pp 12-21.

26. Bullough, V. (2000). *Handbook of Medieval Sexuality*. New York: Garland Publishing Inc.

27. "Law Center: Supreme Court Strikes Down Texas Sodomy Law." (2003, November 18). *CNN*. [Online] URL: http://www.cnn.com/2003/LAW/06/26/scotus.sodomy/

28. Young, D. (1988). *Christianity and the Age of the Earth*. Muskogee: Artisan Publishers.

29. Dalrymple, B. (1994). *The Age of the Earth*. Palo Alta: Stanford University Press.

30. "Genesis Chapter 2 verse 7" in *The Holy Bible: 1611 Edition, King James*. [On-line] URL: www.StudyLight.org

31. Schaff, P. ed. (2006). "Genesis Chapter 2: verse 7" in *The Holy Bible: 1901 Edition, The American Standard*. New York: Thomas Nelson & Sons. [On-line] URL: www.biblegateway.com

32. "Genesis Chapter 1 verse 22" in *The Holy Bible: 1611 Edition, King James*. [On-line] URL: www.StudyLight.org

33. Schaff, P. ed. (2006). "Genesis Chapter 4 Verse 19" in *The Holy Bible: 1901 Edition, The American Standard*. New York: Thomas Nelson & Sons. [On-line] URL: www.biblegateway.com

34. Schaff, P. ed. (2006). "Genesis Chapter 32: verse 22" in *The Holy Bible: 1901 Edition, The American Standard*. New York: Thomas Nelson & Sons. [On-line] URL: www.biblegateway.com

35. Schaff, P. ed. (2006). "Matthew Chapter 5: verse 28" in *The Holy Bible: 1901 Edition, The American Standard*. New York: Thomas Nelson & Sons. [On-line] URL: www.biblegateway.com

36. Schaff, P. ed. (2006). "Hebrew Chapter 13 verse 4" in *The Holy Bible: 1901 Edition, The American Standard*. New York: Thomas Nelson & Sons. [On-line] URL: www.biblegateway.com

37. Palmer, E.H. (1973). "1 Corinthians Chapter 7 verse 30" in *The Holy Bible: 1973 Edition. New International Version New Testament*. Grand Rapids: Zondervan.

38. "Leviticus Chapter 18" in *The Holy Bible: 1611 Edition, King James*. [On-line] URL: www.StudyLight.org

39. "Leviticus Chapter 20" in *The Holy Bible: 1611 Edition, King James*. [On-line] URL: www.StudyLight.org

40. "Leviticus Chapter 11" in *The Holy Bible: 1611 Edition, King James*. [On-line] URL: www.StudyLight.org

41. "Leviticus Chapter 19" in *The Holy Bible: 1611 Edition, King James*. [On-line] URL: www.StudyLight.org

42. "Leviticus Chapter 20" in *The Holy Bible: 1611 Edition, King James*. [On-line] URL: www.StudyLight.org

43. "Leviticus Chapter 24" in *The Holy Bible: 1611 Edition, King James*. [On-line] URL: www.StudyLight.org

44. "Leviticus Chapter 23" in *The Holy Bible: 1611 Edition, King James*. [On-line] URL: www.StudyLight.org

45. "Exodus Chapter 20 verse 13" in *The Holy Bible: 1611 Edition, King James*. [On-line] URL: www.StudyLight.org

46. "Leviticus Chapter 24 verse 17" in *The Holy Bible: 1611 Edition, King James*. [On-line] URL: www.StudyLight.org

47. "Exodus Chapter 31 verse 14" in *The Holy Bible: 1611 Edition, King James*. [On-line] URL: www.StudyLight.org

48. "Exodus Chapter 16 verse 29" in *The Holy Bible: 1611 Edition, King James*. [On-line] URL: www.StudyLight.org

49. "Exodus Chapter 34 verse 2" in *The Holy Bible: 1611 Edition, King James*. [On-line] URL: www.StudyLight.org

50. "Act Chapter 20 verse 7" in *The Holy Bible: 1611 Edition, King James*. [On-line] URL: www.StudyLight.org

51. "Luke Chapter 13 verse 15" in *The Holy Bible: 1611 Edition, King James*. [On-line] URL: www.StudyLight.org

52. "Leviticus Chapter 35 verse 3" in *The Holy Bible: 1611 Edition, King James*. [On-line] URL: www.StudyLight.org

53. "Acts Chapter 15" in *The Holy Bible: 1611 Edition, King James.* [On-line] URL: www.StudyLight.org

54. "Deuteronomy Chapter 22 verse 5" in *The Holy Bible: 1611 Edition, King James.* [On-line] URL: www.StudyLight.org

55. "Deuteronomy Chapter 13 verses 6-10" in *The Holy Bible: 1611 Edition, King James.* [On-line] URL: www.StudyLight.org

56. "Deuteronomy Chapter 21 verses 18-21" in *The Holy Bible: 1611 Edition, King James.* [On-line] URL: www.StudyLight.org

57. "John Chapter 8 verse 7" in *The Holy Bible: 1611 Edition, King James.* [On-line] URL: www.StudyLight.org

58. Cressman, A. ed. (1969). "Matthew Chapter 22 verses 36-40" in *The Holy Bible: 1969 Edition, Worldwide English version. SOON Educational Publications.*

5

The Science Trap

Besides the moral questions of right or wrong, on-going questions exist today concerning the science of homosexuality. What is it? Is it nature or nurture? Is it a choice or genetic? Is it changeable or immutable? Well-publicized funded and unfunded research projects have attempted to answer these questions. Some have clear intent of casting blame. Some have clear motives for eventual behavior modification therapy. Others are simply trying to understand the difference. In this chapter, I will, in layman's terms, explain the more controversial research studies performed thus far; concentrating solely on the data and facts; not my interpretation of the data. I will then critique the conclusions drawn or misconstrued by the media. At the end, I will examine truly where we are at present in the scientific understanding on sexual differences.

It is very recently that legitimate studies have been performed to try and understand homosexuality. In legitimate studies I am referring to replicable, well designed, objective methods; not assumptive-opinion based, or subjective questioning of people possibly under duress or criminals in the justice system.

The Diagnostic and Statistical Manual of Mental Disorders (DSM) published by the American Psychiatric Association, is the handbook used most often in diagnosing mental disorders in the United States. The first edition (DSM-I) was published in 1952, and had about 60 different disorders. Homosexuality was labeled as a psychopathology.[1] Their labeling reflected assumptions derived from legal and religious traditions as well as the psychiatric community's clinical impression. The flaw though of their clinical impression was that the psychiatrists only studied homosexuals who sought psychiatric treatment or who were incarcerated. It was not based on empirical data from homosexual people who were functioning well in society.[2]

When the weakness of these studies became apparent, Dr. Evelyn Hooker, in 1956 conducted a study with two groups of men; both groups neither were not clinically diagnosed mental patients nor incarcerated. The men were matched for age, education and IQ. One group was gay; the other was straight. Using a panel of psychiatrists unaware of the sexual orientation, the men were evaluated. They found most men in both groups to be free from psychopathology, that the ones found to have disturbances not unequal to one group or the other, and using the Rorschach protocol could not differentiate the homosexual from the heterosexual.[3] Dr. Hooker's findings were replicated many times over on both men and women.[4, 5] Overwhelmed with credible empirical data, the American Psychiatric Association, in their 1968 second edition of DSM-II, reclassified homosexuality as a sexual deviancy rather than a psychopathology.[6] Dissatisfied and outraged, gay political activists took umbrage to the negative connation of *deviance*. The argument was that, yes, the lifestyle deviates from the norm, but homosexuality should not be in a text of mental disorders all together. Rightly so, because according to the APA definition of disorder, "distress and social disability",[7] homosexuality did not fulfill the criteria used to define. By 1973 the APA removed homosexuality all together from the Diagnostic and Statistical Manual of Mental Disorders.[7]

Today, in the DSM-IV, there are several groups of disorders: Factitious, Dissociative, Eating, Cognitive, Mood, Anxiety and Substance Related to mention a few. There is also a category of Sexual and Gender Identity Disorders. No, homosexuality did not reappear in the DSM IV. Thank Goodness! But pedophilia, sexual aversion, exhibitionists, sexual sadism and masochism, voyeurism and transgenderism all fall under this category.[8] Ironically, men who boast that they "get off" by watching lesbians being affectionate just voluntarily placed themselves into the DSM voyeurism category.

So we are not sick, but what is the origin of homosexuality? Are we born this way? Is there a gay gene? Is my situation hormonal or environmental? For a clear understanding of the science of homosexuality I feel a need to first run you through brief biology lesson. When you were conceived, 23 chromosomes from your Mom's egg combined with 23 chromosomes from your Dad's sperm. You became a 46 chromosome one celled zygote. All of the 46 chromosomes (or 23 pairs) became nicely centrally organized in the middle of you, the one celled zygote, in an area called the nucleus. You, as a zygote, started replicating rapidly and differentiating into a fetus (unborn baby) with many organs, four limbs, blood cells, muscles, a head, eyes etc. With each cell replication, another 46 chromosome cell was produced. The determining factor of what the cell will look like and its function depends on the turning off or on of particular genes. Genes are instructions for the cell. They are directions for building all the proteins that make our bodies' function. We, as humans, have about 40,000 genes. They determine the color of our eyes, color of our skin, height to a great degree, your sex, even how wide our larynx will be (low our voices will be). Genes are codes on DNA, and the DNA is packaged in unit called chromosomes. Remember the chromosomes I mentioned above? All but our sex cells (sperm/eggs) have 46 chromosomes. Similar to your Mom and Dad, you too have sex cells that only have 23 chromosomes. When they combine with either and egg or sperm they too can help create another 46 cells zygote and the process of maturation begins again.

For clinical purposes, each chromosome **pair** is numbered 1 through 23 based on size and the common gene(s) they carry. For example let's say the gene of eye color is on chromosome 4, then chromosome 4 from Mom carries the gene and so does chromosome 4 from Dad. What color eyes are manifested in you (your phenotype) now depends on which gene, for lack of a better word, overpowers (*cf.* is dominant over) the other. The 23rd paired chromosome is called the sex determining chromosome. Females' 23rd paired chromosome is named XX. The cells in a woman's ovaries divide in half, for reproductive purposes, leaving her with 23 unpaired chromosomes in each egg. Now when the XX split up, she only then has X's to offer each egg. Males' 23rd paired chromosome is named XY. The cells in a man's testes divide in half for reproductive purposes leaving him with 23 unpaired chromosomes in each sperm. Now when the XY split up, he can offer either X or Y in each sperm. Upon ejaculation into the vagina, the 60 million sperm go rushing out and either the sperm carrying an X or a Y can fertilize the egg, housing, as you remember, an X chromosome. If the X sperm reaches first and is engulfed by the egg, then the zygote will be biologically female (XX). If the Y arrives first and is engulfed, then the zygote will be male (XY).

Unless suffering from a major medical structural dysfunction like a hermaphrotic disorder, a XX fetus will have female sex organs like a uterus, paired ovaries, a vagina, and clitoris, and a XY fetus will have sex organs like a penis, paired testes in a scrotal sac, and glands like the prostate and bulbourethral. One's physical sexual appearance or biology is almost standard. The psychological makeup or personality on the other hand, inclusive of sexual orientation, today still marvels researchers. What are the factors that influence or determine personality, behavior, and sexual attraction? Since testosterone or estrogen is the same at puberty between gays and straight, then pubertal hormones is not a factor.[9] Since most parents of gays are both straight, then the heredity factor, home influences (sometimes forcefully), and sexual role models are arguable.[10] If religious and social freedoms or specific cultural influences are factors, then we would not see a homosexuals population, as we do, in every country on this earth.[11]

So much is a mystery concerning the brain of a developing fetus in the uterus, in reference to prenatal hormones secreted by the fetus, chemical makeup of the amniotic fluid in the uterus, the diet and hormones of the mother, and even the so called "essence" of the mother's mental state during the pregnancy. What is for certain is that only a few months after birth most babies develops a sense of noticeable stereotypical maleness and femaleness.

The ultra nurture proponents argue that stereotypical male and female behaviors are environmental, taught, and encouraged behaviors. From birth, babies are conditioned according to them. Boys are dressed in blue and the girls are dressed in pink. Little girls are called pretty and the little boys are called handsome, or both just called cute. Little dolls are put in little girls' cribs while little balls are cribs for little boys. As they grow into toddlers certain toys are encouraged and certain toys are discouraged. Girls are dressed in dresses and the boys in shorts or pants. The hair of most young boys is cut while the girl's is allowed to grow long. Boys are encouraged not to cry and girls are given the freedom to express pain and sorrow through tears. We wrestle with the little boys and exercise delicacy with the little girls. Society conditions the behavior and the personality of their babies.[12] This argument, though, does not account for gender behavioral differences documented numerous times of infant boys and girls who, without external influences, gravitate to certain stereotypically play objects, or without positive or negative reinforcement, display gender typical behavior and personalities.[14]

Despite the social influence, affinity plays a huge role in personality. Parents of some gay and lesbian children reflect back on their child's opposite gender affinity despite opposite influence. For example, although the dolls were given and encouraged, the little girl gravitated to her brother's trucks. Or that the little boy enjoyed playing dress-up with the neighbor's little girl; although he was scolded on that behavior numerous times.

Because some exhibit signs of "gayness" or more accurately, gender nonconformity, when very young against all attempts of conditioning otherwise, many questioned if the child was born with this abnormality. In other words, is it congenital or possibly genetic? Remember congenital simply means born with or present at birth. Congenital can imply so many things outside of actual genes. Genetic means associated with one's DNA and hence could be inherited or can be passed to subsequent generations. It is a part of one's biology with absolutely no way of altering it. The bigger question is, if personality is coded onto DNA or if the brain of an embryo develops in it own unique way predisposing the child to a sexual preference, would twins that share the exact DNA both be gay or both be straight?

Dr. Michael Bailey and Dr. Richard Pillard conducted a study published in 1991 on the prevalence of homosexuality among twins. If indeed homosexuality has a genetic origin, twins who have the exact DNA composition, should show a high if not 100% correlation. They studied 56 pairs of identical twin men where one of the pair was homosexual. They found that 52% were both homosexuals. They also studied 54 pairs of fraternal twins where one of the pair was homosexual and found 22% were both homosexuals. They studied 57 pairs of adopted

brothers where one of the pair was homosexual and found 11% were both homosexuals. He then concluded that homosexuality has a genetic cause.[13]

Two years later Dr. Bailey and Dr. Benishay conducted the study on 147 lesbians with at least one twin or adopted sister. They learned that 48% of identical
twins, 16% of fraternal twins, and 6% of adopted sisters were both gay.[14] There
are many flaws in both these studies. First, environment factors can impact development, where it would be impossible for Dr. Pillard and Bailey to determine
whether it was genetic or environment that caused the twins homosexuality unless
the twins were raised apart. Second flaw is that if in fact genes cause twin homosexuality, one would expect 100% of the identical twins to both be homosexual
instead of 52% with the men or 48% with the females. The third flaw was lack
of repeatability. Many have attempted to repeat this twin study. With disappointment, they found a much lower correlation.[15, 16, 17] Bailey and colleagues even
attempted reproduce this study on an Australian population of twins where one of
the pair was homosexual. The results were that 20% of the male twins were both
homosexual and 24% of the female twins were both homosexuals.[18] Dr. Bailey
himself conceded with this statement, "The essential genetics may not directly
code for homosexuality at all, but something correlated with it," Bailey empha-
sizes. "Something that's advantageous. What is it? We don't know."[19]

Another well known study was conducted by Dr. Dean Hamer of the National
Cancer Institute. He looked at 40 pairs of homosexual brothers and found that 33
of the brothers had the same pattern at the tip of their X chromosome. The other
7 homosexual brothers had different patterns at the tip. He cautiously estimated
that this pattern was responsible for homosexual development.[20] The media took
the statement "responsible for" and had a field day with it. Time magazine July
26, 1993's cover read "BORN GAY Science Finds a Genetic Link" and quoted
Hamer's study.[21] Similarly the Wall Street Journal ran an article titled "Research
Points to Gay Gene" suggesting that a gay-gene has been unmistakably discovered.[22] What they failed to report is the one major flaw. Hamer did not have
a control group; basic to any freshman class science project. In order to make a
statement of difference or deviance from the norm, you must have a norm. In
other words, what does the tip of the X chromosome look like in the heterosexual
brothers of homosexual men? Or, what does the of the X chromosome look like
in heterosexual brothers. The unique pattern seen in the brothers above, could be
a brother phenomenon not a gay phenomenon. For example, if another 40 pairs
of brothers were studied with one of the pair being gay and other being straight,
would they have the same pattern at the tip of their X chromosome? If so, then
you may have valid evidence that the factor involved is that they are brothers.
What should be observed is that the brother's tips are dissimilar in patterns. If
the heterosexual pair of brothers' tips are similar as well, then it can be concluded

that the pattern is a brother phenomenon. No such data was presented nor investigated. Another pressing question is what if any similar pattern is noticed in lesbians. After the publishing of Hamer's article other researchers as George Ebert in Canada and George Rice in Canada attempted duplicate this study and found no statistical evidence that linked a tip pattern of the X chromosome to male homosexuality.[23] In 1999 Wickelgren also reported he too could not verify Hamer's results in studying 54 gay brother pairs.[24]

Dr George Rice was quoted in saying, "Taken together **the results 'suggest that if there is a linkage it's so weak it's not important'**"[24]

A new theory of how sexual orientation develops was proposed by Dr Daryl Bem, a psychologist from Cornell University. He rejected the theory that sexual orientation has a genetic causal element but he supported that it as well as other biological variables such as prenatal hormone may play a role in childhood temperament. It has been well established that pre-adolescence is an extremely influential period; a period that sets the course for the rest of the child's life. According to Dr Bem the temperament of preadolescent girls and boys predispose them to enjoy certain activities. Most boys enjoy competitive sports, getting dirty and play that entail physical exertion; male typical activities. Most preadolescent girls enjoy less physically demanding activities like hopscotch and quiet, less dirty social engaging playfulness like house or dress-up; typical female activity. A small number of boys gravitate to the female typical activities while a small number of girls gravitate to the male typical activities. This affinity is called sex-atypical affinity and the children called gender nonconforming kids. This is as you can imagine a difficult time for these nonconforming kids because the boys are taunted as sissies and the girls considered "yucky' and shunned. This is the point where gender conforming and gender nonconforming kids evolve in a dissimilar a pattern. The children, Ben describes, have, "heightened physical arousal in the presence of peers from whom he or she feels different, unfamiliar, dissimilar and hence exotic." As the child reaches puberty the exotic arousal transforms to erotic arousal and/or romantic attraction. Sex typical children will become attracted to the opposite sex and sex atypical children will become attracted to the same sex.[25] Dr. Bem acknowledges that not every "sissy" boy becomes gay nor does every "tomboy" become lesbian. He does though claim that most do and directs us to a Bailey and Zucker's study showing gay men and lesbians more so than heterosexuals recall gender nonconforming behaviors and interest in childhood.[26] The flaw in Bem's study is negating the 36% of lesbians and 39% of gays who were gender conforming kids. Yes, gays and lesbians may recall gender nonconforming behaviors and interest in childhood more so than heterosexuals, but this study seems to negate the fact that many in the homosexual community are not feminine men or butch women. There are even some in the community who have admitted trying to act like the opposite sex (though it didn't come natural) in order to be socio-sexually compatible with same sex. In order to be with a girl, some girls felt they needed to act like a boy although they were a gender conforming child.[27]

Hormones have, throughout history been publicized as the cause behind homosexuality. The most common claim relating hormones to homosexuality was that gay men had "lower levels of testosterone and higher levels of estrogen in their bloodstream and urine" when compared to their heterosexual counterparts. Same was true about lesbians in that they have a higher amount of testosterone in their bloodstream. Be suspicious when reading articles like these. Unless you have ovaries, you cannot produce estrogen and unless you have testes you cannot produce testosterone. Both sexes have paired adrenal glands though, that produces a steroid hormone called androgen (similar to testosterone). There is a condition called adrenal hyperplasia where the adrenal glands postnatally produce more androgens than normal. This condition causes physical masculinization of a women (body hair, deep voice, enlargement of the clitoris), and causes hyper physical masculinization in men (deeper voice, hairier body, increase genitalia size). Although there is an increase in libido there is no evidence of sexual orientation changing one way or another.

This theory of sexual orientation driven by hormones, which didn't subside until the mid-to-late 1970's, was the driving force for many attempts to cure gay people of their homosexuality. The development of new sensitive hormonal assays now in use fail to show any distinguishable differences between the testosterone levels found in gay males/females and those found in heterosexual males/females. Furthermore alteration in hormone levels in adults by surgical removal of the gonads or hormone injections has failed to induce shifts in sexual preference.[28]

Programs were set up claiming that a cure for homosexuality had been found. Many of these programs incorporated the use of testosterone injections or implants and in the most unusual cases, the implantation of a heterosexual man's testicles, to cure homosexuality.[29] Just recently I was reading the Jamaica Observer and came across an article about an incident in the United Arab Emirates. [30]

DUBAI, United Arab Emirates (AP)—More than two dozen gay Arab men, arrested at what police called a mass homosexual wedding,—could face government-ordered hormone treatments, five years in jail and a lashing, authorities said yesterday.
The Interior Ministry said police raided a hotel chalet earlier this month and arrested 26 men from the Emirates as they celebrated the mass wedding ceremony—one of a string of recent group arrests of homosexuals here.

Hormonal treatment will not cure homosexuality primarily because post natal circulating hormones are not the cause of homosexuality. According to Dr Edward

Stein, "I did not find evidence of a single case where these methods were efficacious. Generally, with the increase of testosterone in the bloodstream, most of the men being treated expressed an increased desire for other men. The object of their affections was not changed at all."[31]

What about prenatal hormones? A number of investigators have suggested that hormonal alterations during prenatal life may influence sexual preference in humans. No human manipulative study though has validated this theory. This well publicized theory was based on a series of rat and guinea pig experiments. Female rodents were given male hormones pre-natally and male were given a steroid hormone to block the effectiveness of his testosterone.[32] The results of this experiment that the general public read and heard about was "the female animal exhibited male sexual behavior during adulthood and the male animals exhibited female behavior during adulthood."[33] Some scientists and certainly the media extrapolated these observations to humans and theorized that when hormones are "dearranged pre-natally" a similar phenomenon in humans will be seen. Flaw number one in this experiment is, without supporting human studies, to make such a statement about humans based on rodents would be absurd. The rodent sexual behavior, by the way, was mating postures. Mating postures in rodents is a rigid endocrine based reflex reaction that can be induced by the investigator through stroking the rodent's back.[34] Humans, as far as I know, do not have a similar sexual behavior. So whether or not our hormones got de-arranged as fetus', human affection cannot be compared to a mating posture.

The most convincing validation (e.g. Money *et al.* 1984, Ehrhardt *et al.* 1985) to a prenatal theory was through observing the childhood and adulthood of people suffering from Congenital Adrenal Hyperplasia (CAH) and Androgen Insensitivity Syndrome (AIS). Please bear with please me again as I again pull you through a brief Biology class. CAH is a genetic disease. Its cause is still idiopathic (unknown). Directly above the kidneys are your adrenal glands. Normally one of the many functions of the adrenal glands is to convert cholesterol to cortisol through a series of enzymatic mediated reactions that are regulated through feedback loops. Deficiencies in one of these enzymes in females (XX) cause an accumulation of a hormone other than cortisol. This "mistake hormone" has properties similar to testosterone and the physical clinical results are enlargement of the genital tubercle (what will become the clitoris), fusion of the internal and external urethra folds (the tube where urine is expelled) and fusion of the labioscrotal folds just as normal testosterone would so in a male embryo. Upon birth, the infant has a marked enlargement of the clitoris and her labia majora and minora (lips of her external genitalia) are fused. As the infant matures and the genitalia remains ambiguous, there is early appearance of pubic and axillary hair, her voice deepens and she will either have abnormal menstrual cycles or not menstruate at all.[35] Studies show that the girl self identifies as female but they engages in stereotypical masculine play; preference to boy toys like cars and gun and a lesser preference to doll and kitchen equipment. They are also been reported to more likely than other girls to accept boys as playmates than fellow girls. As for sexual orientation and depending on the study, homosexual/bisexual orientation (attitude not behavior) ranges from 5% to 37%.[36, 37] About 1 in 14,000 children are born with congenital adrenal hyperplasia.[35]

On the boys side they can also suffer from CAH but no obvious abnormality is present at birth. Remember again we are working with a testosterone-like "mistake hormone". As the infant grows into a toddler, then little boy, he hits puberty way before he is supposed to. Some appear to enter puberty as early as 3 years old. The male child becomes increasingly muscular, penis enlarges, voice deeps and pubic hair appears. Unfortunately the testes are very small.[35]

There is a more applicable disorder called Androgen Insensitivity Syndrome (AIS) where the normal androgen production is suppressed during embryonic development. 1 in every 20,000 births present with AIS. Although the child has male chromosomes (XY) he may be born looking like a girl depending on the severity of the condition (complete or incomplete) In complete AIS only the early non-androgenic aspects of male development begin to take place: formation of testes and early but small production of testosterone. The testes usually remain in the abdomen and can go no further because there no scrotum is formed. No uterus, ovaries and upper vagina form either. The testes make small amounts of testosterone at that point and sexual differentiation does not occur. Most of the prostate gland and other internal male genital ducts fail to form because of lack of enough testosterone. A shallow vagina forms surrounded by normally shaped labia. Phallic tissue remains small and becomes a clitoris. At birth, a child with CAIS appears to be a typical girl, with no reason to suspect an XY child (a boy). Early discovery usually occurs if the child undergoes surgery like surgical repair of an inguinal hernia, appendectomy, or other coincidental surgery. That is when the non-descended testes are discovered. If no incidental surgery is performed, then concern really naturally begins after puberty when the "girl" by the age of 15 does not have her period and has not develop breasts. In performing an ultrasound and hormone analysis, the physician will discover she has no uterus, no ovaries, and that she has an adult male testosterone level because "her" testes are now producing the testosterone as it should.[38] Here is the kicker. Most complete AIS male babies, raised as girls, despite the adult testosterone level, develop adult relationships with men.[39]

Based on these two dysfunctions, a blanket statement was made that prenatal hormones determine the gender identity and sexual orientation of adults.[42] Although my heart goes out to those who may be debilitated socially or emotionally with CAH or AIS, the major challenge I have with the theory of homosexuality caused or attributed to prenatal hormone dysfunction is that, by far, most lesbians do not have any clinical signs of CAH and AIS has nothing to do with most homosexual men. Homosexual men unmistakably look like men. Follow me on this one. If lesbians are lesbians because of prenatal hormones then, by the study, we would have ambiguous genitalia and have issues with menstruation, if menstruate at all. We do not. If gays are gay because of prenatal hormones then, based on the study performed, homosexual men would not have descended testes, a very-very small penis, and upon birth probably mistaken for a girl infant. They are not. A more credible study would show some sort of evidence that a physically identifiable male infant with an irregular suppression of androgen hormones during fetal development growing into an adult man with homosexual tendencies. Or, an infant, with no known physical symptoms, who present at birth with high concentration of androgens, growing into a woman with homosexual tendencies.

A study addressing this type prenatal exposure was conducted by Ehrhardt, and a statement made that "Women exposed prenatally via their pregnant mothers to diethylstilbestrol (DES, a synthetic nonsteroidal estrogen with masculinizing effects in female mammals) *received higher ratings* of homosexual behavior."[41] Although not stated by Ehrhardt and associates, most nonscientists like the Press concluded that homosexual behavior is then *related* to DES exposure.[42] In this study, the 30 women, ages ranging between 17–30 years old had documentation of prenatal DES exposure. These women were compared with 30 women from the same medical clinic. Some of the DES exposed women were also compared with their unexposed sister. 75% of the DES exposed women were exclusive heterosexual in spite of DES exposure; only 1 of the 30 in this study was nearly exclusive homosexual. The rest had at one point in their lives participated in a homosexual act. None of the non-exposed women reported homosexual activity. So although 1 out of 30 is a higher rating than 0 out of 30, be very careful of semantics and what they suggest. Furthermore, it has since been prove than DES neither influences nor resulted in an increased likelihood of homosexual contact.[44]

The last study I will address is one conducted by Simon LeVay and published in *Science*. He claimed that homosexuality has a structural origin; that the hypothalamus (part of the brain that regulates sex drive) of a gay man is different from that of a straight man. Gayness depends of the size of the hypothalamus.[43] When I read this study, I was reflective of another study by Gould in 1982 who published an article with a theory of brain size difference; 9% smaller brains in women. "Women are intellectually inferior to men because their brains are smaller" was the essence of this study.[44] When it was recognized that the brain size is correlated with (relative to) body size as well as the female brain has more densely packed neurons, this notion fell into disrepute.

Back to LeVay. He studied the brains of thirty five men; nineteen homosexuals and sixteen heterosexual. He found that a group of neurons appeared to be twice as large in the heterosexual as the homosexual men. He then suggested that the size of this group of neurons have something to do with sexual behavior. He, after his completion of the study he quoted, *"It's important to stress what I didn't find. I did not prove that homosexuality is genetic, or find a genetic cause for being gay. I didn't show that gay men are born that way, the most common mistake people make in interpreting my work.* "[45] The press went crazy with LeVay's work and reported that "Gay men have smaller hypothalamus."[46]

Gosh where to even start with this one. Weakness number one, his sample size was too low. Less than 20 men in each group is grossly inadequate. Weakness number two, he admitted to colleagues and *Science* magazine that he had to assume the sexual orientation of the cadavers. Subjects were never questioned because they were DEAD!!!. Flaw number three and the most important flaw was that the assumed homosexuals died of AIDS related diseases. We now know about neurological deterioration due to various opportunistic infections.[47] This multivariable study, although still quoted by those who wish to point to hypothalamic causes for gayness, is an invalid study.

So what is the origin of homosexuality? Sorry to disappoint, but we do not know as yet. The quest continues for an answer, or do we really need one.

References

1. American Psychiatric Association. (1952). *Diagnostic and Statistical Manual of Mental Disorders,* (Washington D.C.: American Psychiatric Association), first edition, text revision.

2. Herek, G. (2000). Homosexuality. In A.E. Kazdin (Ed) *Encyclopedia of Psychology.* Washington DC: Psychology Association and Oxford Press.

3. Hooker, E. (1956). A Preliminary Analysis of Group Behavior of Homosexuals. *J of Psych,* 42, 217-225.

4. Bayer, R. (1987). *Homosexuality and American Psychiatry: The Politics of Diagnosis.* Princeton: Princeton University Press.

5. Lingiardi, V. (2002). *The Mental Health Professional and Homosexuality.* New York: The Haworth Medical Press.

6. American Psychiatric Association. (1968). *Diagnostic and Statistical Manual of Mental Disorders,* (Washington D.C.: American Psychiatric Association), second edition, text revision.

7. American Psychiatric Association. (1973). *Diagnostic and Statistical Manual of Mental Disorders,* (Washington D.C.: American Psychiatric Association), second edition, 6th printing.

8. American Psychiatric Association. (2000). *Diagnostic and Statistical Manual of Mental Disorders,* (Washington D.C.: American Psychiatric Association), fourth edition, text revision.

9. Byne, W. Parson, B. (1993) Human Sexuality Orientation The Biologic Theory Reappraised. *Archives of Gen Psychiatry,* 50 (3), 228-239.

10. Lauman, E.O. (2005). *National and Social Life Survey.* Chicago: University of Chicago National Opinion Research Center.

11. Global Information and News. (2000, July 31). *The International Lesbian and Gay Association.* [On-line] URL: http://www.ilga.info/index.html

12. Wharton, A. (2005). *The Sociology of Gender: In Introduction to Theory and Research.* Malden: Blackwell Publishing.

13. Bailey, M. J., and Pillard, R. C. (1991, December). "A Genetic Study of Male Sexual Orientation," *Archives of General Psychiatry,* 48,1089-1096.

14. Bailey, M. J. and Benishay, D.S. (1993). Familial Aggregation of Female Sexual Orientation. *American Journal of Psychiatry,* 150 (2), 272-277.

15. Hershberger, S.L. and Segal, N.L. (2004) The Cognitive Behavioral and personality profiles of a Male Monozygotic triplet set discordant for sexual orientation. *Ach Sex Behav,* 33 (5), 497-514.

16. Joseph, J. (2002). Twin Studies in Psychiatry and Psychology: Science or Pseudoscience? *Psychitr Q,* 73 (1), 71-82.

17. Hynes, J. D. (1995). A Critique of Genetic Inheritance of Homosexual Orientation. *J. Homosex,* 28 (1-2), 91-113.

18. Bailey J. M., et al (2000). Genetic and environmental influences on sexual orientation and its correlates in an Australian twin sample. *J Person Soc Psychol,* 78, 524-536.

19. Blum, D. (1997). *Sex on the Brain: The Biological Differences Between Men and Women.* NY: Penguin Books.

20. Hamer, D. H. et al (1993, July 16). A Linkage Between DNA Markers on the X Chromosome and Male Sexual Orientation. *Science,* 261, 321-327.

21. Henry, W. A. (1993, July 26). Born Gay? *Time.* p. 36.

22. Research Points Toward a Gay Gene. (1993, July 15). *Wall Street Journal.* p. B1

23. Rice, G. et al (1999, April 23). Male Homosexuality: Absence of Linkage to Microsatellite Markers at Xq28. *Science,* 284, 665-667.

24. Wickelgren, I. (1999). Genetics: Discovery of 'Gay Gene' Questioned. *Science,* 284, 571.

25. Bem, D. (2000). Exotic Becomes Erotic: Interpreting the Biological Correlates of Sexual Orientation . *Ach of Sexual Behav,* 29 (6), 531-548.

26. Bailey, J. M. and Zucker, K.J. (1995). Childhood Sex analysis and Quantitative Review. *Dev. Psychol.* 31. 43-55.

27. New, M. (2001). Congenital Adrenal Hyperplasia. In A. Margioris (ed). *Adrenal Disease.* Totowa: Humana Press.

28. Whitehead, N. and Whitehead, B. (1999). *My Genes Made Me Do It: A Scientific Look at Sexual Orientation.* Lafayette: Huntington House Publishers.

29. Fernback, D. (1989, March-April). Biology and Gay Identity. *New Left Review I.* 228.

30. 22 Gay Men Arrested Face Hormone Treatment (2005, November 27). *Jamaica Observer.* [On-line] http://www.jamaicaobserver.com/news/html

31. Stein, E. (2001). *The Mismeasure of Desire: The Science Theory and Ethics of Sexual Orientation.* New York: Oxford Press.

32. Phoenix C. H., et al. (1959). Organizing Action of Prenatally Administered Testosterone Propionate on the Tissues Mediating Mating Behavior in the Female Guinea Pig. *Endocrinology,* 65, 369-382.

33. Carlson, N. (2006). *Physiology of Behavior.* Needham: Allyn and Bacon.

34. Beach F. A. (1977). *Human Sexuality in Four Perspectives.* Baltimore: Johns Hopkins Press.

35. New, M. (2001). Congenital Adrenal Hyperplasia. In A. Margioris (Ed). *Adrenal Disease*. Totowa: Humana Press.

36. Money, J., Schwartz, M., et al. (1984). Adult Erotosexual Status and Fetal Hormonal Masculinization and Demasculinization: 46 XX Congenital Virilizing Adrenal Hyperplasia and 46XY Androgen Insensitivity Compared. *Psychoneuroendocrinology*, 9, 405-455.

37. Zucker, K., Bradley, S., Oliver, G., Blake, J., Fleming, S., Hood, J. (1996). Psychosexual Development of women with Congenital Adrenal Hyperplasia. *Hormone and Behavior*, 30, 300-318.

38. Wisniewski, A. B., et al. (2000). Complete androgen insensitivity syndrome: long-term medical, surgical, and psychosexual outcome. *J Clin Endocrinol Metab*, 85, 2664-2669.

39. Richards, A. (2003). "Androgen Insensitivity Syndrome," *Second Type of Woman*, [On-Line] URL: http://www.transwoman.tripod.com

40. Odent, M. (2006). Genesis of Sexual Orientation—From Plato to Dorner, *Womb Ecology*. [On-line] URL: http://wombecology.com

41. Ehrhardt A. A., et al. (1985). Sexual Orientation after Prenatal Exposure to Exogenous Estrogen. *Arch Sex Behav* 14(1):57-75.

42. Titus-Ernstoff, L. et al. (2003). Psychosexual characteristics of men and women exposed prenatally to diethylstilbestrol. *Epidemiology* 2003:14:155-60.

43. LeVay, S. (1991). A Difference in Hypothalamic Structure Between Heterosexual and Homosexual Men. *Science*, 253:1034-1037, August 30.

44. Gould, S. J. (1981). *The Mismeasure of Man*. New York: Norton.

45. Byrd, D., Cox, S., & Robinson, J. (2001). Homosexuality: The Innate-Immutability Argument Finds No Basis in Science, *The Salt Lake Tribune*, [On-line] URL: http://www.sltrib.com/2001/may/05272001/commenta/100523.htm.

46. Byne, William (1994). The Biological Evidence Challenged, *Scientific American*, 270[5]:50-55, May.

47. Gray, F. et al. (1991). Prominent Cortical Atrophy with Neuronal Loss as Correlate of Human Immunodeficiency Virus Encephalopathy. *Acta Neuropathol (Berl)* 82 (3): 229-233.

50. Di Sclanfani V., Mackay, R.D., et al. (1997). Brain Atrophy in HIV Infection is More Strongly Associated with CDC Clinical Stage than with Cognitive Impairment. *J. Int. Neuropsychol Soc.* May 3(3): 276-287.

6

Developmental Difference

Although neonates (new born babies) can sleep up to 16–20 hours a day, when they awake, they are more aware and competent than they seem. For example, when they have no idea how their own face looks or how to make specific facial expressions, they have the complex ability to imitate the facial expression of adults. If the adult sticks out his/her tongue, open or close his/her mouth, smile or pout, the neonate responds by doing the same. And in doing so, gets positive reinforcement from those around them.

In the first few months of life, adults begin to inadvertently influence and reinforce certain behaviors. As mentioned in the previous chapter, our babies are conditioned and to a certain degree this conditioning influences the personality and behavior of the individual. The question is how much is biological and how much is actual environmental. A French author and philosopher, Simone Beauvoir, in 1940's was quoted in saying, "Women and men are not born, they are made." She was referring to the journey beginning before birth with the pending knowledge of boy or girl, the infant socialization and ultimately the bombardment of external influences that creates male and female.[1] We have moved beyond such early hypotheses to more comprehensive studies embracing various schools of thought. What we do know for sure is that gender is so deeply engrained in society we rarely even notice that our own overt interaction with each other is driven by gender.[2]

We feel a need to know gender of individuals so we know how to act, what to say, and what to expect, and it starts as early as infancy. A myriad of props after a certain age are available so we have no need to ask gender, we just know; facial features, hair length, voice, makeup or lack of, clothing, mannerisms etc. If the props are not there, we, as a society become uneasy. There are so many cases where logically it doesn't matter the gender of a person, but we look for it and panic without it. For example, asking for directions on the street does not require knowledge of male or female, yet an androgynous good Samaritan will wig-us-out, "Hmm was that a man or woman." Does it matter? Well, some say, "Oh, I'm just curious"

But in most cases, that is inaccurate. We feel a need to know so we can adjust our body language, tone, and perceptions. We interact differently armed with that knowledge. How a man asks another man for simple directions is different than how he would ask a woman; and the same goes for a woman asking, even without ulterior motives of overt flirting or sexual intent. With infants it is no different. It has been shown that adults interact differently with infants when provided with the knowledge of boy or girl. We provide different visual stimulation as early as immediately after birth for our own comfort level. In the hospital nursery, after birth either a blue or pink cap is place on the head of the newborn although medical and personal IDs are on the incubator, and the color has no bearing on medical care of the newborn. Similarly, room assignment, nutritional formula, or bedding has absolutely nothing to do with cap color.[2] Apparently we just need to know the gender.

Until age 2, boys and girls exhibit same play behavior, visual acuity and tactile awareness, yet toys, clothing, furniture etc made available are gender typed prior to that.[3] The next time you are shopping for a baby shower gift and asked by the sales clerk if the baby is a boy or girl, say, "It doesn't matter." I almost guarantee a look of total confusion of where to even start in assisting you.

People handle infants more playfully when they believe them to be male and more gently when they believe them to be female.[2] After age 2, boys' and girls' groups begin to diverge as they come to select different toys and engage in different play activities. Parents have been shown to reward or discourage their children's choice of gender appropriate or inappropriate toys respectively. Parents are more excited and engage in active play with the toddler if the activity is gender appropriate. Fathers especially strongly disapprove when male toddlers play with girl toys. He is more likely to ridicule the boy or actually interfere. The same study shows parents only slightly disapproving when a girl plays with a boy toy.[3] Positive reinforcement may build the child's preference on their play. Fathers also have been shown to play rough with boys and gently with girls whereas Moms exhibit neutral play.[3]

By about 3 years of age both boys and girls have develop a *toddler gender identity* in that a little girl knows she is a girl and a little boy knows that he is a boy.[4] At this stage though children have little understanding of what that means. Here at about 3 years old, boys become more active and aggressive and tend to play in larger group while girls talk more, shove less, and tend to interact in pairs.[5]

The controversy still stands with has much of toys and play preference is truly conditioned. A very popular study was conducted where both sex-types toys were made available to children alone in a room unaware they were being watched or judged. Most boys gravitated to the weapons, truck, wagons, and course irregular shaped toys while the most girls gravitated towards the dolls, strollers, smother shaped toys, and kitchen items. Comically, the boys who gravitated towards the strollers threw the dolls inside aside and forcefully and intentionally crashed the strollers into the walls or pretended they were driving a car. The girls used the strollers as transportation for the dolls. Both liked stuffed animals and picture books.[6] When a telephone on wheel was presented to the children, most girls picked up the receiver and started talking most boys pushed around the phone like it was a vehicle. Although a well intended study, it is still unclear how much is based on early influences of the parents. There is a huge debate of toy /play preference and I tend to swing more along the lines of a combined biological-environment theory explanation.

Some like Dr. Gerianne Alexander, Dr Margaret Snow, Carol Jacklin, and Eleanor Maccob believe preference is innate while others like Dr. Yvonne Caldera and Dr. Aletha Huston believe there is a social environmental event that is greatly influenced by parents. Dr. Alexander focused on sex differences in behavior and biological factors. Historically there has been a consensus that masculine toys and feminine toys are clear categories constructed by people and based on society's expectations of gender roles. However increasingly popular is the theory that play-behavior may be more than just what society dictates. There may be something innate that draws boys and girls to different types of toys. Dr. Alexander and colleagues studied vervet monkeys that had no concept of "boy" toys and "girl" toys. Coincidently, they showed the same sex gender toy preference as expected in humans. The young male monkeys spent more time with the balls, bats, trucks, and cars while the young female monkeys play longer with the dolls, towels and pots. Dr. Alexandra concluded that there may be something innate that draws boys and girls to different types of toys. It may be that boys have a natural affinity towards toys to be used actively or propelled through space, and girls to social/ sharing non-aggressive items.[7] Some nonconforming children, though, despite influence, still gravitate to unexpected or "inappropriate" gender toys.

By age 4 or 5 most children know that gender depends on what kind of genitals a person has. They have now acquired *gender constancy* the realization that gender cannot be changed. At this stage also they start to acquire *gender role awareness;* a knowledge of what behaviors are expected of males and females in their world.[4] As a result gender stereotypes are formed. Girls are supposed to be clean, neat and careful, whereas boys are supposed to like rough, noisy physical play. Through cartoons, story books, TV and watching adults in their lives, they come to believe women are emotional, wear pretty clothes, submissive, fuss over their appearance whereas as men are handy with tools, play grown up sports, strong, aggressive and dominant. Idols are pretty ballerinas or fairy princesses (girls) or firemen or the Sheriff (boys). Most exclusive homosexuals do reflect on nonconforming behavior but please note that some do not.

On average, children between 2–5 years old watch over 4 hours of TV or movies a day. They were bombarded with heterosexual themes of boy with girl or man with woman. These themes do not necessarily have to be on the shows themselves, but commercials between sets. When they observe these expressions of affection, what they begin to see as common is boy/girl or man/woman. "Common" quickly becomes "normal". Between the ages of 6–10, kids segregate based on common interests, with the contrasting group viewed as non-compatible and undesirable. I like to call this social apprehension as the "Eww Factor". Typically, in a group of many children you will see many boys with maybe one or two girls in their mist, or a group of girls and a couple little boys in the mist. Teachers and parents start to interfere by forcing the nonconforming children into the group not of their choice. The child is forcefully placed into a group with limited common interests so this child becomes isolated, resentful and withdrawn. It is at this point some gays and lesbians take quite a different road of early development.

Psychologists used to believe that the beginnings of sexual attraction and desire coincided with the physical changes of puberty at the age of 11½ for boys and 12½ for girls, but recent research may be changing this view. Researchers tend to put the first stirring of sexual interest in the fourth and fifth grade (10 years old). It is important however to understand that what ten year olds are experiencing is not adult sexuality. It is mere attraction and not precocious sexuality. Sexual desire and fantasies generally occur much later (1–2 years). This pre puberty attraction is described as a special feeling the kids have for another whether it is a classmate, teacher, neighbor, or movie star. They cut out pictures of them, they write their name over and over again in a notebook, they become speechless and embarrassed around the them, and they call them on the phone a lot just to mention a few. Some report getting shy and giddy. Girls tend to be more vocal and talk about their feeling to friends and parents but boys are more awkward or act out by trying to draw attention (fighting, spiting, yelling), or directly through teasing, pulling of the hair, or hitting.

Remember now that the norm has already been established, so a heterosexual child, although a little embarrassed, feels safe in expressing these new feelings. After all, by then it has been socially pushed on them. When they do express their feelings, they are validated by peers, parents, counselors, teachers, books, TV, video music, and song lyrics. It may even be reciprocated by the crush. For a gay or lesbian child, they enter a stage called "sensitization" or early awareness at age 10. They crush on someone of the same gender. They are aware that this is not "normal" because nothing has prepared them for these feeling. They have been so conditioned by all validations, to get "the feeling" for those of the opposite sex. Never the less, the feelings are there. They too may go through the teasing, writing the names in a book, the calling on the phone phase, and giddy phase, but if it is a straight child the crush is on, oh my Lord, the child's feeling would not be reciprocated. If they talk to their parents about it, they most likely will not reinforce or validate their feelings. The reaction actually may be explosive. Teachers and counselors will advise on the wrongness of the feelings. "Girls are not supposed to like other girls, they are to like boys. Only boys like girls and you are not a boy." The same is said to gay boys. "Boys are not supposed to like boys. They are supposed to like girls. Only girls like boys and you are not a girl". Their friends will call them weirdo, lesbo, fag, sissy, dyke, and puff, most likely tell everyone they can and they may tell *their* parents and so on. The snowball effect may happen to them, or the child may see it happen to one of their classmates. It doesn't take long for the gay or lesbian ten year old to realize what s/he must do; STAY Quiet!! Some actually, still unsure what to do, believe that if they act like the opposite sex, the same sex would like them too. They can slip into depression, thinking that were born in the wrong bodies. Rejection, isolation, teasing, social stunting, low self esteem, loneliness, secrecy, lying, eating disorders, body image issues, suicidal tendencies, and substance abuse could and often follow.

The next stage is *identity assumption*. This stage is where the teenager, with despair, acknowledges their homosexuality. Even with the faking and lying, someone who matters, like a parent or a best friend, may find out their big secret. Family rejection is one of the most painful events in any adolescent's life. If the sexual deception is well crafted, the secrecy spills into young adulthood and possible family rejection may not need to be endured until they are better equipped to withstand the emotional ramification. It still hurt like hell though.

By the age of 15, the child has had much experience of the negativity associated with homosexuality. Religion and society has condemned them. They most likely tried to "change", but realized the impossibility. They may have tried to conform and found the hardship and unhappiness with that. So they contemplate a life of deceit or no life at all. Back in the day (and still in some towns today), there were no support groups, internet help or access, or positive images on the screen, so the adolescent slipped further and further. As the last desperate measure, voluntarily, they may confide in a close friend or parents. Some are thrown out of the home, some are cut off, and some are ostracized. Some just witness the absolute hurt, disgust, and disappoint in the parent's eyes. They hear the words, "YOU ARE SICK!" "You are damned to hell. God will judge you!" "You are an embarrassment and an abomination" "NO, Not my child." "You need help!" Get out, I never what to see you again." Or in my case, "STOP IT NOW before this ruins your life."

"That's it", the child thinks. "I am alone. No one loves me, my life is doomed. I am a freak." In the meanwhile, heterosexuals kids are on their merry way dating, reading their romance novels, flirting, dancing, pre adult courting, getting advice from parents and/or older siblings, and certainly publicly showing their attraction, whether it is holding hands, kissing or cat calling; healthy socio-sexual development, while we are in our hell. Some of us get through this time ok. Few ever experience any hostility (God Bless). Others become totally dysfunctional and self destructive; whether through cutting (self mutilation), heroin, cocaine, crack, marijuana, alcohol, suicide attempts, seek prostitutes/gigolos, rest stop anonymous sex, and get wrapped in a harmful codependent relationship. Also it doesn't take a genius to realize that the conventional place to meet other gays and lesbians is at an exclusive bar or club; not at church, not in the grocery store, not at school and not at work. The vices (tobacco, alcohol, party drugs) are prevalent at the bars so that can too lead to dependencies.

As children, believe me when I say that, if we could change or "stop" our situation we would have. But we couldn't and still can't, so we have no alternative (less of living a miserably deceitful life) but to accept our homosexuality and fight for the right to live healthy safe lives. One of the very reasons (besides the political and social protest) we march and hold parades is for a one day celebration of expression otherwise stifled year round by the societal distain. One day out of the year we can get together in numbers and let loose. Heterosexuals in their sexual privileged world can not and should not dare judge us until they have walked in our pebble filled shoes.

References

1. Bair, D. (1990). *Simone de Beauvoir: A Biography*. New York: Summit Books.

2. Eckert, P., & McConnell-Ginet, S. (2003). *Language and Gender*. New York: Cambridge University Press.

3. Langlois, J. & Downs, A. (1980). Mothers, fathers and peers as socializing agents of sex-typed play behaviours in young children. Child Development, 51, 1237-1247.

4. Stoller, R. (1994). *Sex and Gender: On the Development of Masculinity and Femininity*. Oxford: Taylor and Francis Group.

5. Maltz, D., Borker, R. (1982). A cultural approach to male-female miscommunication. In John Gumperz (Ed.), *Language and Social Identity*. Cambridge: Cambridge University Press. pp. 196-216.

6. Caldera, Y., et al. (1989, February). Social Interactions and Play Patterns of Parents and Toddlers with Feminine, Masculine and Neutral Toys. *Child Devel,* 60 (1), 70-76.

7. Alexander G., & Hines, M. (2002). Sex Differences in Response to Children Toys in Non-Human Primates (Cercopithecus Aethiops Sabaeus). *Evolution and Human Behavior*, 23, 467-479.

7

Crimes Against Gays and Lesbians

[We] walked outside the bar and there were about six guys standing on the corner down from the bar. Our car was parked right on the corner of where they were. As we were walking towards them, they saw us coming and started walking towards us. They started calling us "fags," saying "fags," "look at the fags" and "nigger fag." ... They said "We're going to kill us some faggots today" and "we don't want fags in [this city]".... They attacked us with bricks and clubs. [My friend] was hit in the head with a brick, and when he went down, they hit him more in the head with bricks and clubs till he stopped moving. I was hit in the legs with a club, and broke my knee cap. The other two friends got away and went back into the bar to call the police, and came out with more people from the bar, and chased the attackers away until the police got there. The police took about 20 minutes to get there and the ambulance almost a half an hour. By that time [my friend] had already expired. He died in my arms.[1]

Local, state, and federal crimes are viewed from a legal perspective which takes as its starting point the statutory definitions contained in the laws enacted by the government. A crime is a crime not based on the harm caused, grave discomfort, humiliation, common sense of what not to do, or inappropriate behavior, but it is a crime because the law says it's a crime. It was a crime in Nazi Germany for Jews to walk on the "German" sidewalks prior to then being deported and relocated to the ghettos; resistance to such in itself was a crime as well. Harboring or helping to emancipate a human being who fled a deplorable situation; a situation where s/he was kidnapped from their country, forced to work without compensation, and treated inhumanly was a crime in the United States of America. The crime was not the institution of slavery but rather the fight to dissolve it. With that said, keep in mind that a crime is a crime when the law says it is a crime.

Progress has somewhat been made and there are laws forbidding certain violent crimes like rape, assault and murder, and assigning punishment if a crime is committed. Under the Civil Rights law, specifically the 14th Amendment of the U.S. Constitution, Section 1:

"All persons born or naturalized in the United States, and subject to the jurisdiction thereof, are citizens of the United States and of the State wherein they reside. No State shall make or enforce any law which shall abridge the privileges or immunities of citizens of the United States; nor shall any State deprive any person of life, liberty, or property, without due process of law; nor deny to any person within its jurisdiction the equal protection of the laws."

In other words, we are protected by law against crimes. Every violent crime *should* be prosecuted to the fullest extent of the law. It should, but it is **not**. Let us take a glance back into history when the 14th Amendment should have protected all Americans.

Violence against people of color reached a head in the 1960s. Crimes directly targeting African Americans ranged from rapes, beatings, hangings, shootings, stabbings, intimidation, vandalism, and hurtful propaganda. Authorities turned a blind eye. Some authorities even encouraged and participated in the crimes themselves. If the criminals were brought to justice (which few were), many of the cases were dismissed, or, if convicted, punishment was minimal. In most cases the jurors determine the guilt or innocence of the defendant. Even if all possible evidence showed with no shadow of a doubt that the defendant committed the crime being tried, still the jurors controlled the outcome or the verdict, and it was that jury or public opinion that released human right offenders. At the time, there was no federal recourse for the victims. Over time black leaders and civil rights activists took action, and with much fight and visible protest, were instrumental in getting Hate Crime Legislation passed in 1969.

Hate crimes are crimes such as violent acts, hate speeches inciting violence, or vandalism that are motivated by feelings of hostility against any identifiable group within society. At the time the legislation was passed in 1969, it served only to protect race, religion, and natural origin, and applied only if the victims were engaged in one of six protected activities:

1) enrolling in or attending a public school

2) participating in a service or facility provided by a state (voting)

3) engaging in employment by any private or state employer

4) serving as a juror

5) traveling in or using a facility of interstate commerce

6) enjoying the services of certain public establishments

Crimes motivated by hatred toward particular groups not only harm the individual victim but send a strong message of discrimination and intolerance to all members of the group to which the victim belongs. Because of the effects, hate crimes rightly so carry a harsher punishment. One who can be moved to violence by hatred of a class of people presents a greater danger to society than one who merely hates an individual. The individual victim of a hate crime typically did nothing to provoke the attack and is therefore interchangeable, at least from the perpetrator's standpoint. I would like to call these crimes *mass intent* but the Canadians have an official term for actions of this sort; *advocating genocide.*[2] Genocide is legally defined as "with intent to destroy in whole or in part any identifiable group", namely:

a)   Killing members of the group, or

b)   Deliberately inflicting on the group conditions of life calculated to bring about its physical destruction.

It is not unusual to make state of mind a distinguishing element of a crime and the punishment suitable or appropriate with culpability. Homicide, (or the death of a human being by someone other than the victim themselves), is not just a homicide. There is first degree murder, second degree murder, criminal involuntary manslaughter, criminal voluntary manslaughter, and non criminal manslaughter. There are nonviolent crimes like scienter and fraud with the distinguishing factor being if the perpetrator knowingly or unknowingly (state of mind) defrauded the victim. Laws are subjective not absolute, and society determines if one crime deserves more punishment than another based on the motivation.

When a homosexual or a transgender is a victim of a violent crime, often, not always, it is because of his or her sexual orientation or gender identity. Such crimes, motivated by bigotry, are not like other violent crimes. Insult to injury is that crimes against transgenders, lesbians and gays are not always taken seriously, because law-enforcement officers, emergency medical workers, like some members of society, are often unsympathetic, if not downright hostile.

A case in point was an inexcusable event that occurred in Washington D.C. in 1995. Tyra Hunter born Tyrone Michael was a transgender woman. On August 7, 1995 she was injured as a passenger in a car accident. District of Columbia Fire Department arrived on the scene and started administering care. Firefighter and Emergency Medical Technician Adrian Williams, once he discovered Tyra's male genitalia, withdrew life saving medical care and for 7 minutes uttered derogatory epithets at her. He was quoted in saying, "This ain't no bitch. He's got a dick and balls". In the emergency room, Dr. Jospeh Bastien neglected to provide Tyra with blood which was at that point available. She died. At the trial, medical experts testified that Tyra had a 86% chance of surviving if provided with proper medical treatment. Although her initial injuries were not a result of hate crime, her death was. On December 11, 1998, after a five-week trial, the jury awarded Margie Hunter, Tyra's mom, approximately $2.9 million in damages. The jury determined that D.C. Fire Department employees violated the D.C. Human Rights law, and that Tyra Hunter's death was caused by medical malpractice. In announcing the settlement, the Mayor of D.C. at the time Anthony Williams said, "discrimination by officials or employees of any agency of the District of Columbia Government based on race, gender or sexual orientation, of the nature alleged in this case, will not be tolerated." D.C was one of the few states to include sexual orientation in their state hate Crimes Statutory provision.[3]

In the United States, the prevention, investigation, and prosecution of crimes against persons or property-whether or not bias-motivated-is primarily the responsibility of local authorities. The federal role is limited but nonetheless crucial, with federal authorities serving most often as a backstop when local efforts to address bias crimes issues fail.

To date (Spring, 2007) three states have no hate crime laws, sixteen states have hate crime laws but do not include sexual orientation protection, and 30 states have hate crime laws that include sexual orientation.

States w/ no hate crime laws	States having hate crime law but exclude gays, lesbians, and bisexuals	States having hate crime laws inclusive of gay, lesbians and bisexuals
Indiana, South Carolina, Wyoming	Alabama, Alaska, Arkansas, Georgia, Idaho, Michigan, Mississippi, Montana, North Dakota, North Carolina, Ohio, Oklahoma, South Dakota, Utah, Virginia, West Virginia	Arizona, California, Connecticut, Delaware, Distinct of Columbia, Florida, Hawaii, Illinois, Iowa, Kansas, Kentucky, Louisiana, Maine, Maryland, Massachusetts, Minnesota, Missouri, Nebraska, Nevada, New Hampshire, New Jersey, New York, Oregon, Pennsylvania, Rhode Island, Tennessee, Texas, Vermont, Washington, Wisconsin

There have been two attempts in 2001 and in 2004 to amend the current federal hate crime law to include homosexuals. It has taken until September of 2005 for the legislation to pass, extending Hate Crime Laws to include gays, lesbians, and transgenders. As an amendment to the Children Safety Act, the measure received bipartisan House of Representative support, passing on a 233-199 vote, later to be stripped from legislation that year. In 2007 the House again passed the Law Enforcement Hate Crime Prevention Act on 237-180 vote, and although the Senate may too vote in its favor, President George W. Bush vehemently opposes the bill and pledges he will veto it. The primary responsibility still rest with the state and local officials.

The opponents to this bill argue that allowing homosexuals protection under federal hate crime laws give them special consideration that is not warranted. Not warranted??

Well, here are the hate crime statistics from the Federal Bureau of Investigations (FBI). According to the report, "Hate Crime Statistics, 2005" incidents reported in 2005 involved 7,163 offenses and 8,804 victims. The report indicated 2005 hate crimes fell into the following categories:[4]

- Racial bias 54.7 percent (3919 offences)
- Religious intolerance 17.1 percent (1227 offences)
- Sexual orientation 14.2 percent (1017 offences)
- Ethnicity/national origin 13.1 percent (944 offences)
- Disability less than 1.0 percent (53 offences)

Please remember that the 1017 sexual orientation offences above are not crimes specifically against homosexuals. The number represents crimes with have clear cut, well-established indicators and parameters (see list below) that the attack on the person was based on his or her sexual orientation; whether homosexual, bisexual or heterosexuals. By the way, the FBI plum does not track crimes against transgenders. Their numbers do not even fall into the homosexual category.[5]

According to the 2005 hate crime statistics, anti homosexuals offenses accounted for 971 of the 1017 sexual orientation offences listed above. Anti-heterosexual offenses accounted for 21, and anti-bisexual for 25. In other words, 95% of the attacks were anti-homosexual driven. In the gay community though, we believe the numbers to be higher, in that the FBI bases its statistics on compilations of crime data by state and local enforcement agencies. Gays and lesbians have traditionally not reported crimes to the police because of fears of being outed or that the police will not pursue the cases.

On the racial bias side, anti-black accounted for 2630 of the 3919 racial bias attacks, anti-white 828 anti-Asian 199 and anti-multiracial 183. On the religious intolerance side, anti Jewish offences accounted for 848 of the 1,227 offences, anti-Catholic-58, and anti Islamic-128.

Granted there are millions of criminal offenses in the U.S. every year that are not motivated by hatred toward a particular group. Mostly they are pursued and the perpetrators punished to the fullest extent of the law. But again, hate crime legislation protects not only individuals but entire communities victimized by prejudice. At this point in history the communities most under attack are the Blacks, gays, lesbians, transgenders, Jews, Muslims, Native American and the Amish, but the law protects all communities not just the ones most under attack.

Case 1: On September 22, 2005 Jean Beizaire forcibly struck a 17 year old female to the back of her head. He, a black male, admitted striking her because she was white. He was initially charged with battery which is a misdemeanor, but because it was a hate crime it became a felony.[6]

Scenario 2: After seeing a woman kissing her husband goodbye at the train station, three gay men sporting tanks tops with "ALL BREEDERS MUST DIE" displayed, followed her, calling out "you nasty breeding whore," dragged her into an alley, viscously tore out her hair, savagely crushed the tips of her fingers, broke both ankles, and left her battered and naked in a dumpster. This is not just an assault, this is a hate crime.

The point is hate crimes are not special treatment or legislation for Blacks, Gays, or Jews etc., but protection legislation for even those groups that are not typically victimized like whites, heterosexuals, and Methodists.

Although legislation does not address the verbal intent and slander due to the 1st Amendment (freedom of speech), it sends a clear message that genocidal behavior and intimidation behavior such as property damage, vandalism, assault, arson are not acceptable from anyone.

How does law enforcement and legal community determine whether a crime is a hate motivated crime? The following questions are asked.[7]

- Were the offender and the victim of different racial, religious, ethnic/national origin, or sexual orientation groups?
- Would the incident have taken place if the victim and offender were of the same race, religion, ethnic group, or sexual orientation?
- Was the incident provoked?
- Were bias-related drawings, markings, symbols, and/or graffiti left at the crime scene?
- Were certain objects, items, or things which indicate bias used or left behind by the offender(s)?
- Was the victim engaged in activates promoting or indicating his/her racial, religious, ethnic/national origin, or sexual orientation group?
- Is there another clear motivation for the incident?

- Were any racial, religious, ethnic, or sexual orientation bias remarks made by the offender??

- Were there any offensive symbols, words or acts which are known to represent a hate group or other group or other evidence of bias against the victims group

- Did the incident occur on a holiday or other day of significance to the victim's group or the offender's group?

- What do the demographics of the area tell you about the incident?

References

1) Herek, G. Cogan, J., & Gillis, J.R. (2002). Victim Experience in Hate Crime Based on Sexual Orientation. *J. of Social Issues*, 58(2) 319-339.

2) Department of Justice Canada (2006, September 15). Hate Propaganda. *Consolidate Statutes and Regulations: Criminal Code (R.S. 1985, c. C-46):* Author.[On-line] URL: http://laws.justice.gc.ca/en/C-46/280838.html

3) Gay Men and Lesbian Opposing Violence (2006). *Homophobia in the District of Columbia Fire Department.* Gay and Lesbian Activists Alliance Inc. [On-line] URL: http://www.glaa.org/archive/1996/glovfire.shtml

4) United States Department of Justice: Federal Bureau of Investigation (2006) *Uniform Crime Reporting Program Hate Crime Statistics 2005.* Clarksburg, WV: Author. [On-line] URL: http://www.fbi.gov/ucr/hc2005/table1.htm

5) Najafi, Y. (2004, December 3). FBI Reports Spike in D.C. Area Hate Crimes. *Washington Blade.* Washington D.C.

6) Latest Student Arrested at Sandlewood Charges with Hate Crime (2005, September 22). *News4Jax* [On-line] URL: http://www.news4jax.com/index.html

7) United Sates Department of Justice: Federal Bureau of Investigations. (2005). *Training Guide for Hate Crime Data Collection.* Clarksburg, WV: Author. [On-line] URL: http://www.fbi.gov/ucr/traingd99.pdf

8

Same Sex Marriage

Definition

Humans are naturally driven to term-identify, quantify and categorize the world around them, and this is why the precise definitions of objects and practices vary contemporarily and historically between and within cultures. What something is called and defined as today over here may be different to what is it called and defined as over there, or years from now. Definitions vary because they are not absolutes, and this is where the real debate needs to begin. Before we get trapped in an ostrich approach to the world, we need to start asking why. In other words, why is a word defined as such? What exactly is a definition?

A definition merely serves as a guide. It serves to standardize an understanding of the world as we know it. As we evolve as a species, technologically, scientifically and socially, we become more aware of not only the hypocrisy of certain definitions but more importantly we become aware of our limitations. Definitions are time and knowledge sensitive. The fight for freedoms has its roots buried in the act of questioning. For every debate, if we ran to a historically antiquated piece of documentation for a definition, we would hit a wall of social and political stagnation. Advances in health care, education, and community tolerance all have their roots too buried in the act of questioning the status quo or conventional definitions. Why does a car need to run on **petroleum**, as an initial definition of a car was? Why is the head-of-household a **man**, as the original definition was? Why does a table have **four vertical legs** and a flat surface? Why is an attorney **a man** who practices the profession of legal representation? Why is a nurse **a woman** who assists in the recovery of the infirmed, and why is life defined as the presence of **a natural pulse**? You see, all these outdated definitions are based on *form* and not much emphasis on *purpose*. Does the table have to take a form of four legs, or is a table serving the purpose of a flat utility surface? Form is based on the limitation of our present knowledge base or unexplored possibilities. In many cases, we can still satisfy the purpose while expanding the form, and in some cases when the purpose itself has evolved, so MUST the form. We have found that a car can run on solar energy, a woman can be a principle breadwinner, a man can impart compassionate assisted care for the sick, a structure firmly attached to a wall with no legs can be called a table, a women can litigate a case and uphold the constitution of the U.S, and some believe that life (although still hotly debated) begins at conception without the heart yet being developed.

Some sources, like the Encarta Encyclopedia, describe marriage as a socially recognized and approved union between individuals who commit to one another with the expectation of a stable and lasting intimate relationship.[1] Most sources, like the Webster's Dictionary, define marriage as a life long union between a man and a woman. Proponents of gay marriage challenge this contemporary absolutism of a man and a woman. Now there is little debate that the majority of the world is heterosexuals; having attractions to the opposite sex and wanting to have sex with the opposite sex, but why were legal stable unions made between one man and one woman in the first place? Historically, did the pair actually care about each other so deeply to want to spent the rest of their lives together, or was there another explanation for being institutionalized into a legal pair. One explanation for this union takes a pragmatic approach. In the past, men were the sole economic leaders of the community, and women, and the children they bear, were dependent on these men. Women entered into unions for economic reasons more so than emotional reasons.[2] Food, shelter, protection, and reliable sexual outlet, most likely superseded love when these unions were formed. Marriage was done out of duty, obligation, and necessity. Much of the time both man and woman didn't know each other prior to their wedding day.

Also, if unmarried at a certain age, both men and women were treated as outcasts, viewed as poor providers, or socially ostracized. Agrarian villages of the past prospered with many hands in the field. They were better fortified to defend against attacks with many residents, and they were certainly insured of lineage continuance with many offspring. Prosperity, security, and continuity could only come about with procreation. Another important element of marriage hundreds of years ago was the establishment and maintenance of peace through the joining of families from different tribes. But today, really, why do people marry?

Marriage or Holy matrimony has been a sacrament when practiced by Christians. In Catholicism the Sacrament of Matrimony is between three people: God, man and woman. I respect such a practice but am not blind to the fact that legally you still need that marriage license to be permitted to marry and a marriage certificate issued by the state as proof of marriage, not necessarily the blessing of the church.

Although constitutionally there is a separation of church and state, government hypocritically is still influenced by the doctrine of the church. They claim same sex marriage is immoral without a justifiable reason outside of biblical alliteration for such a stance. In arguments against gay marriage, the Bible is sure to be used to defend normality and righteousness. Since this is the case, I will first quote the biblical reasons and arguments, and later in the chapter I will address the social and legal reasons why marriage *has to be* opened to gays and lesbians by shear logic.

According to Ephesians, the first purpose of marriage is oneness.[3] The Bible also espouses that marriage is for "the generating and nurturing of offspring, indissoluble union, mutual help of spouse and the remedy of concupiscence (powerful feeling of physical desire).[3] The Christian conservatives hold firm to the first of these, screaming that marriage is between a man and a woman so they can bring forth children; conveniently ignoring the other aspects like the fact that it *is* dissoluble based on the 45–50% first marriage divorce rate, 60–67% second marriage divorce rate, and 70–73% third marriage divorce rate. Many partners *are not* well supported based on the 4,000,000 domestic abuses each year, and marriage *doesn't remedy* concupiscence based on the wide prevalence of adultery.[4, 5] According to a survey conducted by the University of Chicago National Opinion Research Center, 25% of all men had been unfaithful and 17% of women.[6] In many cases, marriage is not even necessarily wrapped in love but rather publicity. Let's tackle the first argument that marriage must be and is linked with the fundamental right of procreation.

Nature and Procreation

Marriage is the traditional venue within which children are conceived and reared. The contention is that gays and lesbians who seek same sex marriage cannot procreate, it is unnatural, and they should be denied the right to marry. Unnatural??? Based on what, nature? Animals and plants do not marry. Marriage in itself is unnatural. The accepted responsibilities of marriage include a social union, sexual exclusivity, a mature, sound decision of livelong commitment, and security, yet only about 3% of the 4,000 mammalian species live is social pairs and none are exclusively monogamous. That is the misconception of the phrase *mate for life*. Mate for life means animals mate with each other for a life time but not exclusive with each other in their live time. Beavers, otters, bats, wolves, coyotes, some foxes, a few hoofed animals, and some primates are some of the mammals that live together in social heterosexual pairs. You would be surprised to learn that many mammals, fish and birds live in social homosexual pairs. Yes, they pair off heterosexually to breed, but much of their sexual activity involves both sexes. Long term bonding involves the same sex. Courtship displays, affection, and rearing of the young involve the same sex. This phenomenon is not due of mistaken identity. The differences between the sexes are obvious; body shape, color, scent, and size are dead give-aways. So, suffice it to say that these animals pair up heterosexually for procreative reasons, but for companionship (sex included) they pair up with the same sex. Does this type of behavior sound familiar? "So, what are these animals?" you are probably asking yourself. To date there are 478 different species that exhibit some form of homosexual or bisexual behavior observed both in the wild and in captivity. It is evidenced by behaviors listed above (sex, courtship, affection, pair-bounding, and parenting). The species vary from birds, to mammals, to fish, to insects. Here are some mammalian examples: whales, sheep, lions, deer, raccoons, elks, bears, tigers, giraffes, kangaroos, elephants, dolphins, zebras and chimpanzees. The avian examples are owls, penguins, turkeys, galah, parrots, teals, egrets, doves, ostriches and swans. Finally, here are some fish examples: salmon, sunfish, jewel fish, and stickbacks. Well-known books written by Paul Vasey, Frans deWaal and Bruce Bagemiehl outline the various animal homosexual behaviors and how each of the species flourishes in the mist of the diversity.[7, 8, 9]

So in choosing to use animals as comparative beings, and in choosing to use such terms as natural and unnatural, be careful what nest you stir. You may indeed find out that marriage is actually unnatural and homosexuality actually natural although not as common as heterosexuality. Three to ten percent of humans are said to be gay; ten percent of the silver gulls display homosexual activity, eleven percent bisexual activity; nine percent of the Japanese macaques display homosexual activity, fifty six percent bisexual activity; and a hundred percent of the bonobo chimpanzees display bisexual.

Procreation does not define a marriage. If procreation is the essential goal of marriage, then postmenopausal women and men with erectile dysfunction would be banned from marrying. The same applies to partners where one or both are sterile or impotent. They are allowed to marry though aren't they? Yes they are. Therefore couples, where procreation is impossible, *have* the right to marry. This principle was upheld in *Griswold* and *Turner* cases, where the Supreme Court rejected that procreation is the dominant goal of marriage but rather, "the unitive goals of equal companionship, mutual support backed up by law and expression of love and commitment."[10, 11] If procreation were to be the essential goal of marriage aren't we putting children (to later be conceived) at risk in allowing convicted pedophiles and child molesters to marry; which all 50 states allow?[12]

So again, why do people marry? Some want to start families, yes, but, the overriding purpose of most 1st world marriages is to be together; physically and sexually; something that actually can be accomplished without benefit of the law. Another intangible benefit is the social insurance. Social insurance is personal between the couple, and is a type of insurance against bad times; where a spouse is required to provide financial and emotional support when things are going badly ("for better or for worse, for rich or for poor, in sickness and in health"). If one spouse is impaired, the other is trusted to be both caretaker and decision maker. Being married is a legal status with many tangible benefits; legal rights and benefits automatically associated in a one shot deal, which I will address later in the chapter. So why can't a law abiding adult couple, who love and respect each other, committed to a life long equal companionship with each other, wishing to support each other emotionally and financially, and desiring social recognition as a couple marry and enjoy the legal benefits as such? I'll get back to that.

The Slippery Slope Argument

Not just anyone can get married, as you know. There are limitations on marriages that are upheld by individual states and by the federal government. These limitations fuel the slippery slope argument that many ultraconservatives use; "if we allow same sex marriage, must we also recognize bigamous, incestuous, and child marriage?" No you don't. They are two different issues, two different fights. Imagine if the argument on the floor of Congress on giving women the right to vote went as such "Well if we give women the right to vote, we must also give children, foreigners, and criminals the right to vote too!" Absurd right? Children are not of age, foreigners are not American citizens and should not have a say in the laws that bind us as Americans, and federally convicted criminals lost their civil rights when sentenced. As voting rights, there are limitations on marriages and more importantly there are arguable, sensible reasons behind these limitations. Homosexuals do not wish to have more than one spouse, we do not wish to marry relatives, and we certainly do not wish to marry children.

Not so long ago most states in America upheld the ban on marriages of different races; especially those between European and Africa descendent couples. Brave advocates of mixed race unions took their fight to the state and federal courts demanding justification for such a prohibition. The courts could not find legitimate justification for races to remain separate in marriage despite the constitution amendment lobbying to keep it so. In that case, marriage was a race issue, and in granting interracial marriages did not mandate recognition of gay marriage now did it? Both were unrelated. If the law grants or legalizes a practice, let say practice A, based on principles that also all applies to practice B, then it must recognize practice B as legal. The converse is true in that if the law denies a practice, let say again practice A, based on a principle that also applies to practice B, then it must include practice B as banned as well. Now, there are defendable reasons for the restrictions put on all bigamy, incest and child marriages, and whether you agree with these reasons is irrelevant, the arguments have no bearing on homosexual adults fighting for the right to marry.

Bigamy Argument

Men still hold more economic and political power than women in this society so most bigamous marriages would take the form of polygamy rather than polyandry (a woman marrying more than one man). In a polygamous marriage, the central goals (companionate and social insurance) of marriage have been argued to be compromised.[12] The emotional bond between husband and wives are diffused, spousal benefits are questioned and fragmented, inheritance, legal rights to children and decision making responsibilities when the husband is incapacitated seems to frequently be in question. There is not a single decisive voice. Some argue that polygamy would put men at a disadvantage in that an excess of single men would be in competition for a limited number of available women.

Under an anti-bigamy law, a married man cannot marry a second wife. Many get around that law by marrying and divorcing many women with a clear understanding that his ex-wives will keep his last name, cohabitate with him, and socially be united with him, sharing him with the rest of his ex-wives. Legally, though, unless legally authorized, only his recognized civil wife reaps spousal benefits and is considered next of kin.

A constitutional decision on an adult **monogamous** gay marriage would have no effect on state regulation of bigamy. The argument against polygamy does not pertain to same sex marriage. By law, to grant one does not grant the other. They are unrelated principles.

Incest

Although procreation is not the primary purpose for marriage (we have established that), heterosexual marriage still lends itself for *possible* procreation. The first issue the layperson thinks about when they hear *incest* is mutant babies, right? The second issue is probably father and juvenile daughter or brother and sister having hot sex. So let's address these points.

The harmful recessive genes argument in incestuous cases is unsupported today because it has been well proven that in most incestuous couples, recessive gene problems are extremely slight and unimpressive.[13] The chances are exponentially unlikely for a harmful outcome. As a matter of fact, incestuous breeding has been shown more to strengthen the organism rather than weaken. Previously held notions were that harmful recessive genes would pair up and produce defects in offspring. That is not the case. Ironically unrelated heterosexuals with diagnosed dominant genetic defects (a 100% probability of hereditary transfer) are allowed to marry despite this line of reasoning.[12]

So dismissing the gene argument, the main contention today against incestuous marriage is that, if a child comes from this union, his/her sense of socialization would be affected. "For the process by which each generation reaches beyond the family unit and forms new one is very useful for society and perhaps necessary for the individual as well."[12]

A large amount of incest cases, not rape cases, involve men and their adult daughters, not juvenile daughters. Many believe though, although certainly not substantiated, that those fathers manipulate and seduce their daughters when they are children, and rather than focusing on platonic child raring are more focused on their future sexual ulterior motives, truly demonizing the relationship. The point is that proponents argue that once the child becomes an adult, they can make mature decisions on with whom they wish to have a committed, lifelong-intended, sexual relationship. Whether it is a biological unmarried parent, step parent or adoptive parent, is irrelevant.

The thought of brother and sister marrying is terrifying to parents and the community as a whole because they visualize a courtship as children, and imagine premature sexual exploration when unsupervised. Brothers and sisters live and play together and have much unsupervised time together. Parents and society would like to trust that type of relationship. Even as sibling adults, people still view with disgust such a sexual relationship. "Yuck, they know each other too well." Curious, wouldn't you say? Isn't *knowing* someone a positive?

The challenges in the incestuous marriage laws are in the cases of adult relatives who wish to marry and not breed, or adult step-relatives where none of the previous arguments of genes and nuclear family apply. There was a case in Wisconsin where the state court denied a marriage license for two adult adoptive siblings.[12] What a ludicrous ruling, and one I would not champion. As a matter of fact, this is an issue I believe we must also visit in the future and I for one will stand in favor for modifying the incest laws. That is not the issue at hand though. As explosive as incest issues are, note that incestuous marriage laws are not absolute. All fifty states and the District of Columbia (D.C.) prohibit brother-sister, parent-child, aunt-nephew, and uncle-niece marriages. Only thirty eight states prohibit first cousin marriage. D.C. and eleven states prohibit step relatives marriages. Two states (Louisiana and Alaska) prohibit persons within four degrees of consanguinity (relationship by blood), and one state, Utah, prohibits 5 degree of consanguinity; the same state that has been petitioning for the ban of polygamy to be lifted. In other words, Utah wants to legalize polygamy which means many women may be bearing children from only a few men. The chances of being related just increased multifold.[12, 14] Hmm??—Wow, do the math on that one. Instead of having a class of 30 children from 30 different mommies and 30 different daddies, you will have 30 children where there are 30 different mommies and 10 different daddies if each dad takes 3 wives. The chances then are greater to meet someone related to you. But the matter at hand is that we as homosexuals are not violating the incestuous limitation to the marriage laws. In simple terms, our partners are not related to us. Recognizing adult monogamous same sex couples the right to marry has no effect on the incest regulation. By law, to grant one does not grant the other. They are based on unrelated principles. The courts need to provide a rational reason for denial.

Child Marriage

Marriage is one of the most important emotional and economic decisions most people make in their lives. A bad decision can be extremely costly. Empirical as well as casual evidence demonstrate that adolescents are immature decision makers.[15] Children may not be mature enough to make such important decisions as marriage. That is why there are well justifiable age of consent laws. To assure a mature decision, the state requires parental input, or requires the children to wait a few years. Gay and lesbians do not have that luxury. Like with incest, state limitations on marriage laws are not absolutes when it comes to children marrying. Children *are* allowed to marry under certain circumstances. In all fifty states 17 years olds can get married if a parent's consent. Forty-nine states, under those same circumstances, allow 16 year olds to marry. Forty states allow fourteen year olds to marry. Nine states allow children under 18 to marry without parental consent if the female is pregnant with the male.[12] A resolution recognizing a constitutional right for same sex **adult** couple to marry would have no effect on state regulation of child marriage.

To further perpetuate the ban on gay marriage argument, some imbeciles start pulling at straws saying, "if you allow gays to marry you will have people wanting to marry their pets or their cars." Should I even grace that with an explanation? Ah, what the hell. Some people may need an explanation. Pets are animals, not humans, with no objective or fundamental way of communicating their consent or intensions to the courts. They may not offer the financial support nor do they have decision making ability if and when needed. As for a car; a car, by law, is not a life form; even a Lamborghini. For the love, people grow up!! Still people hold to the only thing they can to deny us a marriage license. "Marriage has to be between a man and a woman." My Gosh, WHY? What I am trying to say is that there is no legal justification to ban same sex marriage.

Still No!

There are many who say, "If you allow *those people* to marry it will undermine and disgrace the institution of marriage." Well, there are so many ways to look at this argument. Let's first look at the premise, the institution of marriage. Those who argue under this principle should take a hard look at what marriage has become with no help from homosexuals. The right wingers and ultra conservatives do not use the word *institution* as a *custom* or *practice* because marriage customs and practice change every year both in the church and in the court room. It was practice to be married only by the clergy, custom for races not to intermarry, or for the bride to be in white. That's not the issue now. They are referring to the wholesomeness and sacredness of marriage. Watch them the next time you hear them utter those words, *"the sanctity of marriage.* They knit their brow, articulate their words, dip their voices, and hand gesture to emphasize the piety of their words. They raise marriage up on this pedestal of divinity. Now in the Church, matrimony is still definitely a ceremonious event where premarital classes are attended and a blessing of God and church is bestowed upon the couple. A couple can be blessed all they want, but without that piece of paper, a state marriage certificate, they are not legally married.

Marriage of the heart and soul is a personal evolution and many, including myself, embrace such a union, but the truth of the matter is that legally getting married is merely obtaining a marriage license, having an official perform a ceremony, obtaining the certificate after the ceremony, and then reaping the benefits and rights there after. Today, one doesn't need to be able to fulfill the responsibilities of what a marriage should be; love, cherish, honor and most importantly 'till death do you part. That is not in question these days. What is being questioned is the gender of those in love. The concept of marriage is what has gone into the crapper. Marriage, I believe, is the vow you take, the promise you make, and the responsibility you must uphold. All decent adults who are willing to uphold these vows should be considered for marriage.

To get married in Maryland both the man and the woman need to be 18 years old or older. With no appointment necessary, both must go together to the county clerks office and bring with them official identification and proof of age. Depending on the county, they will pay between $35 and $60 and give under oath that their full name, place of residence, age, and social security numbers are correct. They need to then affirm under oath that they are not married to anyone else. No blood test is required. Next is to schedule a ceremony with the deputy clerk, pay $25 dollars, and return in at least 48 hours. A ceremony can be performed by the deputy clerk, a judge or someone from a religious order.[16] In Florida, a notary public can perform the ceremony.[17] There is no set format, script or protocol for what needs to be asked or said. The certificate is signed by the man and woman, signed by two witnesses, and, Viola, they are married.

It is extremely idealistic to think of this process as independently sacred, because it is harder to get a drivers or hunting license than a marriage license. The process is very easy, cheap, and has the lowest standards of any license. The couples are not even asked if they like each other when filing an application for a license.

What is this great institution of marriage anyway? An institution that allows convicted rapists and murders to marry with no questions asked; an institution that allows convicted child molesters and pedophiles to marry; an institution that has no preparatory course or test of competency; an institution with almost a 50% failure rate. Marriage was intended to be a permanent institution. Historically, legally grounds for divorce had to be circumstances that justified making an exception. The spouse seeking a divorce had to prove that the other had committed one of the faults (cruelty, adultery, or desertion) recognized as justification for the dissolution. As of 1969, every state in the union grants divorce without proof of fault. It is called the no fault divorce law. Marriage is no longer viewed as a covenant. It's now an unreliable, poorly drafted contract. Even in a loose business contract, the law holds that a specific promise is binding and cannot be broken merely because the promisor changes his or her mind as does in marriage. The impact of the institution of marriage has been devastation yet divorce law is not called into question or held accountable. Gays are not the problem.

Marriage is intended to be wrapped in love, respect, honor, and protection but it is an institution riddled with spousal abuses. As a matter of fact 25% of all crimes is wife assault and 2/3 of all marriages will experience internal violence at least once. Domestic violence occurs in over 60% of marriage is the United States.[5] Those who have once or multiple times over proven that they cannot abide by the rules and responsibilities (martial duties) like sexual monogamy, emotional and financial support, respect, and LOVE (hello), are allowed right back in. Swingers, those in a marriage who swap sexual partners, are allowed to remain in the institution. Yet when a couple wants "in", so legally two separate lives can become one, who actually know and love each other, who are adults, who are unrelated, who have for many years adhered to the obligation of sexual fidelity, who provide support to their mate, who may want to love and support children, and who have no criminal records are denied. You must again ask why. There definitely needs to be marriage reform, but to chastise couples who can uphold obligations of a marriage is not where the attention should be targeted.

"Homosexuals *demean* marriage?" This statement is assuming that the love and commitment heterosexual couples share is worth more than what is shared between us. That is false, as well as extremely presumptive. How the heck can one measure degree and depth of love and affection? We love as deep as any heterosexual couple if not deeper. Furthermore, once a commitment is made, we are no more or less likely to commit adultery or infidelity. There is no supporting data proving either case, so please do not assume the worse on us. Our love is real and valid. As for sex, good gracious, I would not have the faintest idea of where to get legitimate comparative data on such a personal topic of sexual gratification and orgasmic intensity. I can only speak from personal experience and for my circle of friends in both communities. Having sex, making love, indulging in intimate ecstasy with the person of your desires is so real, so magnificent, so fulfilling that nothing compares. Do not minimize the love and passion homosexuals feel for each other.

So what is the reason to deny same sex marriages again? You cannot deny on the grounds that it is unpopular or distasteful to some. That opens the legal flood gates of discrimination no matter how one looks at it. In a community that Asian and Caucasian unions are unpopular or distasteful, would they be denied a license? Yet we are denied for reason of distastefulness. The justification for prohibiting same sex marriage boils down to prejudice against gays and lesbians.

I find myself asking why even get married and be a part of this *rotten* <facetious> marriage club riddled in hypocrisy. Well it ultimately comes down to social acceptance of the union and most importantly, is the slough of automatic legal privileges that follows. A spouse is truly, in the eyes of the law, viewed as the ultimate significant other and the most important person in the life of the other. There is no getting around it. A spouse holds more social credibility than a "special friend."

According to the U.S. General Accountability Office there are 1,138 federal laws from which married people profit.[18] Upon obtaining a marriage certificate here in United States, a couple **automatically** has many rights including but not limited to the following:

1) Next of kin privilege
2) Bereavement leave
3) Shared taxes
4) Wrongful Death benefits
5) Pension and health insurance
6) Immigration rights
7) $100,000 to spouse of any public safety officer killed in the line of duty
8) Social Security benefits
9) Child custody rights
10) Legal immunity from testifying
11) Accidental death benefits

12) Division of property after dissolution of marriage

13) Legal status with partners children

14) Right to sue for tort and death by wrongful act

15) Rights to involuntary hospitalization

16) Funeral leave for government employees

17) Making, revoking, and objecting to anatomical gifts

18) Permission to make arrangement for burial and cremation

19) Tax relief for natural disaster losses

20) Joint parenting rights, such as access to children's school records

21) Family visitation rights for the spouse and non-biological children, such as to visit a spouse in a hospital or prison

22) Domestic violence intervention

23) Marital recognition in every state of the union and internationally

To illustrate these rights, I feel compelled to explain and give some examples.

Next of Kin Privilege—Next of Kin is the term used to describe a person's closet living relative. When a spouse is living, automatically s/he supersedes all blood relatives as next of kin, where no clear will or instructions have been given. Following the spouse, next of kin are children, parents, siblings and grandparents, in that order. Next in-line are uncles, aunts, first cousins, and so forth down the blood family. Next of kin privilege is mostly utilized when concerning inheritance and in making decisions when there is a medical emergency.[19]

There is a legal term not commonly used in everyday conversation. That word is *intestate*. Intestate means dieing without a will. Most people do not have a will. If a person dies intestate, statutes confer rights of inheritance and property on a widow or widower; property and inheritance greater than the sum of his or her enforceable debt and funeral expenses. This includes real estate, stocks and bonds, cash (bank account), vehicle(s), boat(s), furniture, electronics, jewelry, business interest, pension, IRA, 401K etc.[20]

If and when a person falls severely ill and can no longer make medical decisions, the spouse, being next of kin, can step in and make these important decisions if no living will exists. If unmarried, the adult child, parent or sibling can step in. The same goes for making funeral arrangement. Once gay and lesbian couples make a life together, they are not privy to these rights. If one partner dies, blood family can step in and take everything of the deceased if in the deceased's name although property was built together as a couple. I knew a woman, "M", whose life partner "K" of 8 years was brutally shot and later died. Her (K's) family are Seven-Day-Adventist and never approved of K's lifestyle nor of M. Unfortunately because M had credit issues, their business was in K's name, so was their bank account and their home. Upon K's death, the family took their home and business; even the computers, then turned around and pressed charges against M for trying desperately to empty their bank account (by signing K's name). No matter how long same sex couples are together or what commitment was made between them, they are not entitled to their partner's property after death. Even if the immediate family is respectful of the relationship, a homo-hater second cousin can actually step in and take all they have built together.

Another example is one of a devoted couple (Dan and Paul) of 29 years. For 33 years, Dan had been estranged from his family. His family never approved or supported his lifestyle and vehemently said they wanted nothing to do with him or his devilish ways. Dan expressed to Paul on several occasions that he did not want to be left on life support if ever brain dead. Well, Dan was involved in a serious car accident that crushed his skull leaving him indeed brain dead. Due to his condition and the possibility that Dan may pass, Paul immediately contacted his family. When the prognosis was presented to Paul, he voiced that Dan wanted not to be put on life support. The family stepped in demanding that he stay on life support and used Dan's and Paul's estate (what was in Dan's name) to pay for medical bills. After 2 years on life support, when assets were exhausted, they then decided to take him off. Paul had no legal voice.

Once again, when a partner dies intestate, a spouse has automatic next of kin privilege. Therefore homosexual life partners all need to draft wills in order to secure their place as beneficiaries and their power of attorney or health care proxy in medical emergencies; as well as carry these documents when traveling just in case one of them becomes ill or has an accident. The legal fees for wills and time involved are major inconveniences let me tell you. All said and done, the will can still be challenged by the family; and usually is. This process is just one of many legal annoyances that a same sex couple has to endure. The next few examples, bereavement leave, shared taxes and wrongful death benefits, are completely independent of the couple's legal efforts.

Bereavement Leave—Most federal and private companies are required to have certain policies in writing and honored by their Human Resources Department. Matters concerning sick leave, maternity leave, workman's compensation and funeral leave are standard. Federal law requires that companies allow all full time employee three days off to attend or make funeral arrangements if a death occurs in the immediate family. This is paid time off, by the way. The immediate family includes spouse, parents, stepparents, siblings, children, stepchildren, grandparent, father-in-law, mother-in-law, brother-in-law, sister-in-law, daughter-in-law, son-in-law, or grand-child. Companies most often do require proof or verification of kinship.

Homosexual employees do not get the time off if their life partner dies and are completely at the mercy of their employer to grant them the time. If their life partner dies and the funeral is on a weekday, there will be obvious challenges or possibilities of being fired in taking the day to say good bye providing that the employee has no saved sick or vacation days.[21] Imagine a wife not being able to say goodbye to her husband? Or have I not convinced you as yet that the depth of love shared between the two and the hurt of loss are no different?

Shared taxes—Married couples can file federal income tax return jointly. In combining both incomes, the tax rate between them most likely will be lower and if not itemizing deductions, the standard deduction could be higher. In other words, the lower the tax rate and the higher the deduction, the more earned money you keep.[22]

Wrongful Death Benefits—Wrongful death is when a death is caused by the negli-gence of another. It may not be criminal in nature so no arrests are made. In addition to the emotional hell caused by the sudden death of a loved one, there are financial burdens put on them as well; especially on partners in a two income household; not to mention the medical bills prior to death. Spouses and immediate family can file suit and seek compensation to cover loss of support or companionship, men-tal anguish, lost benefits, lost wages including future earnings, medical and funeral cost, and lost inheritance.[23] Life partners just have to grit and bear the loss.

John Langan's life changed forever when his gay civil partner, Neil Conrad Spicehandler, was struck by a hit and run driver. He was immediately sent to a Manhattan hospital for treatment of his broken leg. After Spicehandler's leg was operated on a second time days later, Langan got a call that his partner was dead. Langan and the family successfully sued when the hospital was unable to satisfactorily explain how minor surgery led to death.

In appeal, the New York Court of Appeals ruled that Langan had no right to sue since he and Neil Spicehandler were not married.

Larson's attorney, Adam Aronson told the Associated Press, "If this decision is allowed to stand, same sex couples will be denied the very significant and important protections that all married heterosexual spouses can get. And they will be denied those protections for no reason other than the fact they are gay."[24]

Visitation Rights—Many hospitals limit visitation solely to family members (spouse included as family). For gays to be granted permission to see their partners they require *hospitalize visitation authorization* in writing and they must have it on their person when traveling. If not, they may be denied access.[23] There was a case:

(BALTIMORE, February 27, 2002)—Told by hospital staff in Baltimore that he could not visit his dying life partner because he was not the partner's family, Bill Flanigan, a resident of San Francisco, today sued the University of Maryland Medical System in Baltimore City Circuit Court. Flanigan's partner of five years, Robert Daniel, had been admitted to the medical system's Shock Trauma Center in Baltimore on October 16, 2000, from complications arising from AIDS. Flanigan and Daniel were on their way to visit Flanigan's sister in the Washington, D.C. area, where a nearby hospital transferred Daniel to the Shock Trauma Center—part of the University of Maryland Medical System—because of Daniel's critical condition.

As he was kept in the waiting area of the Shock Trauma Center, Flanigan asked staff members to allow him to see Daniel and to confer with Daniel's physicians. They told him only "family" members were allowed to do so, and that "partners" did not qualify.

Flanigan explained he had a Durable Power of Attorney for Health Care Decisions and that he and Daniel were registered as domestic partners (in California). The Shock Trauma Center also had the records of the first hospital to which Daniel was admitted, where Flanigan was recognized as family, having spent the night in a chair by Daniel's bed.

The Shock Trauma Center acted quite differently. For four hours, personnel kept Flanigan away from Daniel and his doctors—meanwhile allowing family members of other patients to visit their loved ones and confer with doctors. Flanigan, on the other hand, was not given the opportunity to make surgeons aware of Daniel's wish not to have life-prolonging measures performed on him, including the insertion of a breathing tube.

After four hours, Daniel's sister and mother arrived from out of town. Only then did the Shock Trauma Center provide information on Daniel's status that had been repeatedly denied to Flanigan, and subsequently allow the entire family, including Flanigan, to see Daniel. By that point, Daniel was no longer conscious, his eyes were taped shut, and the two men never had the chance to say goodbye"[25]

So many ask, "would you gays be satisfied with a domestic partnership law or civil union?" The answer is as such. Some in the community say "we do not need this stupid marriage law nor the civil union or domestic partnership to validate our love. We are married in our hearts and that's all that matters". I respect although may not agree with those taking such a complacent stance. They have just deprived themselves of possible public recognition and all civil rights as a couple. They, in the eyes of the law, are just another pair of close friends or lovers. Some may have an attorney draw up papers to grant the partner legal rights to certain things, but it costs thousands of dollars in legal fees when a simple marriage license / certificate, costing under $100, would cover all the same rights and benefits. Not too many of us have that kind of money, and the shear injustice of the disparity pulls us into the fight for marriage recognition. As mentioned above, any of these papers drawn up can be challenged in court. Gosh forbid if you show up at the hospital without your paperwork or if the hospital personnel disregard the paperwork for whatever reason. In a life and death situation, there needs to be a clear understanding of what role you as a same sex partner play, and let us not forget, time is of-the-essence.

Domestic partnership entitled some economic benefits like in California where domestic partners are granted the ability to have custody of a partner's child, access to family court, the right to make funeral arrangements and access to married student housing.[26] Other places like Multnomah County, Oregon have grossly limited rights and responsibility although partners can register as domestic partners.[12] Domestic partner rights differ from municipality to municipality and not recognized outside of their jurisdiction. Domestic partnership is also not limited by the rules of divorce.

Civil unions offer some of legal protections and benefits of marriage but less than half of the 1,138 benefits available to heterosexual married couples. Exempt from civil unions are benefits like sick leave to care for an ailing partner, immigration rights for partners who are foreigners, federal benefits such as survivor benefits through Social Security, tax breaks, veteran's benefits, insurance breaks, and many many more.[12]

The few protections granted through civil unions also do not extend beyond the borders of the state from which it was given, and no federal protections are included with a civil union. Marriage laws, on the other hand, have the possibility under the standardization of the Full Faith and Credit Clause of the U.S. Constitution to be nationally and internationally recognized. Getting married for some is a momentous event with participation from friends, family, and the community. Supposedly, it is the pinnacle of a commitment, and in marrying, a couple has proclaimed that fact to the world that they and their spouse are more than close friends but rather soul mates and only in death shall they part.

Four sovereign nations, Netherlands, Canada, Spain and Belgium, recognize same sex marriage. South Africa in December 2005 by a ruling of 9 to 1 charged that "the country's marriage laws unfairly discriminate against same-sex unions." The South African courts have given lawmakers one year to amend the country's marriage act.[27] In the United States, the state of Massachusetts has legalized same sex marriage. That's great but the Supreme Court enacted the Defense of Marriage Act in 1996 that made sure that the Federal government and other states need not recognize the union.[28] Only three states, Connecticut, New Jersey and Vermont, opened civil union status to gays and lesbians. The following states have domestic partnership status for same and opposite sex couples: Colorado, California, Hawaii, Maine, Alaska, New York and D.C.[28]

So what is the hold up? First of all, civil marriages are governed by state law. Providing that a marriage is consistent with State and U.S. Constitutions, each state sets the conditions for a valid marriage and the conditions by which it is dissolved. Although states have the primary regulatory power where marriage is concerned, the federal government has occasionally regulated the terms of marriage like in the case of bigamy and miscegenation (interracial marriage). In 1967 the Supreme Court stepped in and ruled that all bans on interracial marriage were unconstitutional for example. At the time, 16 states were still enforcing this ban. Advocates for prohibiting interracial marriage (and there were many) used words like divine law, immorality and unnatural union. Unbelievable!!

States need not recognize a civil marriage certificate granted in another state if it challenges the limits of the state's constitution. Back in the 1960s states like Virginia, Maryland, North and South Carolina, Louisiana, and Missouri would not acknowledge the legal marriage of a mixed race couple within their state borders. The same applies today with same sex marriages of Massachusetts.

The present antigay government of this countries and the Supreme Court itself cannot "ban" gay marriage based on unconstitutionality because it is not unconstitutional. So they have tried to change the constitution so it would be. As you remember this was voted down in 2004 and 2006. Thank goodness the bigots couldn't make and still cannot make a legal case. It was dismissed not because they suddenly agreed with or condoned our lifestyle. The senate failed to approve the Federal Marriage Amendment. In order to be a part of the Constitution, the amendment would first have to be approved by 2/3 majority in both the Senate and the House of Representative., and then ratified by at least ¾ of the U.S. state legislators.

The government legally couldn't justify their prejudice. In other words, immoral how? Unnatural how? Wrong how? No legal answer so far can be rendered because there is no legal answer. What ex-president William Clinton did do in 1996 was to propose an act which later passed called the Defense of Marriage Act (DOMA). DOMA defined marriage on a federal level as a union of one man and one woman. He completely overrode the Full Faith and Credit Clause of the U.S. Constitution. Again what that means is that even if a state like Massachusetts legalizes same sex marriage, the federal government would not honor it. The Full Faith and Credit Clause, also called Article IV Section 1 of the United States Constitution, when enacted in the late 1700's, was intended to provide continuity or comity between states and enforcement across state lines of non-federal laws, court rulings and civil claims. So to recap, States can govern what constitutes a civil marriage. If what they decide doesn't sit well with the federal government, the government can disregard it, even if they cannot make a case of why disregarding it is just. Furthermore, the government through DOMA can ensure that all states need not recognize a legal marriage. If government believes it is the right thing to do, they can vote under the Full Faith and Credit Clause to standardize it. They have not in the case of same sex marriage. The government chose the road of deprivation and hatred. That's where we are today. Institutionalized prejudice.

Popular opinion is changing and a new generation of open minded citizens are springing up while the narrow-minded straight supremists are passing on. Many liberals, moderate conservative, Christians, Jews and atheists are looking beyond our sovereign borders to culturally thriving nations who have adopted positions of inclusion; all doing very well. Tolerance rather than intolerance is on the rise, and people are stepping away from conventionality into positive possibilities. My hope is that the federal government will repeal the Defense on Marriage Act so marriages, in states that have allowed same sex unions, will be recognized as such by all the states of the union. Also I pray that the federal government will, as in 1967 with miscegenation, declare that all bans on same sex marriage to be discriminatory and hence, illegal. We need all Americans who embrace equality to help make this a reality.

Please try and not see gay and lesbian marriage or our lifestyle as moving in the direction of immorality. We are not immoral people and how we live our lives is not immoral. Homosexuality is just uncommon to the populace. That's all. We gays are not the enemy. We will not tarnish the principles of marriage, only make it stronger with our love, respect and commitment for each other. Instead of confined to the absolutism of a man and a woman, what should marriage be? I have an answer for you. Are you ready? Here goes, 'a sexually exclusive and equitable love relationship entered into voluntarily by two adults celebrated by vows and recognized by themselves, the courts, and others as the highest romantic achievement possible between two people and only in death asunder.'

References

1. Marriage. (2006). *Microsoft® Encarta® Online Encyclopedia*. [On-line] http://encarta.msn.com

2. Graff, E.J. (2004). *What is Marriage For? The Strange Social History of Most Intimate Institution*. Boston: Beacon Press.

3. Schaff, P. ed. (2006). "Ephesians Chapter 5 verses 22-31" in *The Holy Bible: 1901 Edition, The American Standard*. New York: Thomas Nelson & Sons. [On-line] URL: www.biblegateway.com

4. Hurley, D. (2005, April 19). Divorce Rate: Its Not as High as You Think. *The New York Times*.

5. Women's Rural Advocacy Programs: Statistics About Domestic Abuse. (2003, October 17). *Lets Wrap*. [On-line] URL: http://www.letswrap.com/dvinfo/stats.htm

6. Schrof, J. (1998, August 31). Adultery in America. *U.S. News World Report*. p. 31.

7. Vasey, P., Sommer, V. (2006). Homosexual Behaviour in Animals: An Evolutionary Perspective. Cambridge: University Press.

8. deWaal, F. (1997). *Bonobos: The Forgotten Ape*. Berkley: University of California Press.

9. Bagemihl, B. (1999). *Biological Exuberance. Animal Homosexuality and Natural Diversity*. New York: St Martin Press.

10. Supreme Court of the United States. (1987). William R. Turner et. al. verses Leonard Safley et. al. Court Case 482 U.S. 78. [On-line] URL: www.en.wikipedia.org/wiki/turner_v._safley

11. Supreme Court of the United States. (1965). Estelle T. Griswold and C. Lee Buxton verses Connecticut. Court Case 381 U.S. 479. [On-line] URL: www.en.wikipedia.org/wiki/griswold_v._connecticut

12. Eskridge, W. (1996). *The Case for Same Sex Marriage: From Sexual Liberty to Civilized Commitment*. New York: The Free Press.

13. Bratt, C. (1984) Incest Statutes and The Fundamental Right to Marriage: Is Oedipus Free to Marry? *Family Quarterly* vol. 18.

14. Llewellyn, J. (2004). *Polygamy Under Attack: From Tom Green to Brian David Mitchell*. Scottsdale: Agreka Books.

15. Caukfman, E., Steinberg, L. (2000). (Im)maturity and Judgment in Adolescence; Why Adolescents May be Less Culpable Than Adults. *Behavioral Science and Law* vol. 18 pp 742-743.

16. U.S. Marriage Laws: Maryland. (2006). *United States Marriage Laws*. [On-line] URL http://usmarriagelaws.com/search/united_states/maryland/index.shtml

17. U.S. Marriage Laws: Florida. (2006). *United States Marriage Laws*. [On-line] URL http://usmarriagelaws.com/search/united_states/florida/index.shtml

18. United States General Accounting Office. (1997, January 31). Table of Statutory Provision Involving Marital Statutes to the United States Code. *Defense of Marriage Act GAO/OGC-97-16.* Washington D.C.

19. Next of Kin. (2006, October 20). *Wikipedia.* [On-line] URL http://en.wikipedia.org/wiki/Next_of_kin

20. Intestacy. (2006, October 4), *Wikipedia.* [On-line] URL http://en.wikipedia.org/wiki/intestacy

21. AClU Answer Gay Marriage: Should Lesbian and Gay Couples be Allowed to Marry. (1998, June 30). *American Civil Liberties Union.* [On-line] URL: http://www.aclu.org/lgbt/relationships/11845res19980630.html

22. Dolan, E.M., & Stum, M.S. (2001). Economic Security and Financial Management Issues facing Same Sex Couples. In Jennifer Lehman (ed) *Gay & Lesbian Marriage and Family Reader: Analyses of Problems and Prospects of the 21st Century.* New York: University of Nebraska Press.

23. Curry, H., Clifford, D., & Hertz, F. (2004) *A Legal Guide for Lesbians and Gay Couples.* Berkley: Delta Printing Solutions Inc.

24. Simpson, A. (2005, October 13). Gay Partner Can't Sue Hospital for Malpractice, N.Y. Appeals Curt Rules. *Insurance Journal* [On-line] URL http://www.insurancejournal.com/news/east/2005/10/13/60829.htm

25. Chauncey, G. (2004). *Why Marriage? The History Shaping Today's Debate Over Gay Equality.* Cambridge: Basic Books.

26. Domestic Partnership (2006, November 2) *Wikipedia.* [On-line] URL http://en.wikipedia.org/wiki/Domestic_partnerships_in_California

27. Gay Marriage Around the Globe. (2005, December 22). *BBC News.* [On-line] URL http://news.bbc.co.uk/1/hi/world/americas/4081999.stm

28. Marriage/Relationship Recognition (2006) *Human Rights Campaign.* [On-line] URL http:// www.hrc.org

9

History / AIDS

History

Sexual and emotional companionship with the same or both genders is not a new phenomenon. This behavior was openly expressed during and documented in the Middle Ages, Renaissance and expansion eras, in many different cultures, and by many distinguished and admired people. People such as Julius Caesar, Plato, Socrates, Aristotle, Leonardo Di Vinci, Cary Grant, Johnny Mathis, Malcolm Forbes, Tennessee Williams, Marlon Brando, Leonard Bernstein, Rock Hudson, Billy Holiday, Tony Curtis, Bessie Smith, Richard Chamberlain, Susan B. Anthony, Alan Turing (the father of Computer Science), and many others are/were either gay or bisexual.[1, 2] In Native American cultures, many respected women took on male social roles as head of household, warrior and provider, and took as their sexual partners, women.[3] In China, before Jesuit Christian missionaries gained influence, nearly every emperor in the Han Dynasty had one or more male sex partners. It is also believed homosexuality was popular in the Song, Ming and Qing Dynasties.[4] In Japan during the medieval period, love between men was viewed as "the purest form of love". Even today, despite the influence of Western thought on its culture and attitudes, Japanese law still includes no specific prohibitions against same-sex activity.[5]

Homosexuality has a rich history of acceptance but also equally a grim history of non-acceptance. For example, in 1533, due to King Henry VII's proclamation that any non-procreative sexual activity was a crime, he outlawed masturbation, anal sex, fellatio and cunnilingus. Many men and women were burned, mutilated and hanged for their "crimes" on account of that law.[6] Being a colony, America was governed by similar British law. In America in 1649 Sarah White Norman and Mary Vincent Hammon were convicted in Massachusetts of "lewd behavior with each other upon a bed" and both humiliated and sentenced to prison time and hard labor; making this the first documented conviction in the New World for homosexuality.[7]

Jumping ahead 300 years to the middle of the 20th century, gays remained closeted with the fear of being arrested or harmed. If suspected to be gay, one was harassed, assaulted, denied employment, deprived of their children, denied access to public places (theater, restaurants, amusement parks, etc), housing, and health care. During this time, secret meeting social places were established, usually bars, and the phenomenon of dressing in drag, impersonating heterosexual couples, was common. The McCarthy era of the 1940's and 1950's was not only marked with banishment of suspected communists from public office, cinema, fashion, and the literary arts, but there was a nationwide witch hunt to rid the country of homosexuals as well. This was an awful time for gays and lesbians. There are some who still have not recovered from the harmful slander and complete destruction of their lives and careers.[8] The time was not yet ripe for an uprising. Gays had no political power and no economic clout as we, although limited, have today. It was not until the "Stonewall Riots" when the community as a whole ignited with the fighting mantra of "No more!!" meaning no more are we accepting the blatant injustice and bigotry this country is feeding us; no more will we keep invisible; no more will we stay quiet. The uprising of June 28, 1969 was actually not a "riot" by the true sense of the word. It was more along the lines of a rebellion with one major element absent; more organization. A riot by definition is where a crowd of people gather and are committing crimes, whereas a rebellion is an act or show of defiance toward authority or established convention.

The Stonewall Inn was a popular meeting place for gays in Greenwich Village, New York. At the time, gay bars were frequently raided, patrons harassed, and some charged with indecency of some form or another. Names, address, and occupations of those arrested were published in the newspaper as well. In New York, in 1969 public show of affection was not a crime, so that was not the recorded reason for the raid at the Stonewall Inn. Some say it was shear harassment under the legal premise that the Stonewall Inn was operating and serving liquor without a valid liquor license, that there were links to organized crime, and nude entertainment was rumored to take place there (and that was a violation of indecency laws).[9] An interesting catalyst to the escalation of the unrest was that a few days before, Judy Garland had died. Now, Ms. Garland was an extremely important cultural icon with whom many in the gay community identified. She was an actress and singer with much pizzazz, along with a sordid life of pain and disappointment. She was embraced by the gay community because of her vulnerability and strength as well as her failed marriages with the two gay men. Her father apparently was also gay, go figure.[10] Although she was found dead in Chelsea-London, UK, her interment took place in New York City on the same day, just, a few hours before the uprising. Of the 22,000 attendees to her funeral, 12,000 were gay men. That evening it is said that the patrons of the Stonewall Inn were distraught, and the grief and anger of her untimely death at age 47, contributed to the lack of passivity when the raid started.

On the first night only 13 protestors were arrested. On the second day, 400 police officers were called in to squash the uprising and approximately 2,000 gays, lesbians, transgenders, and transsexuals kept the electricity of the night at a feverish high. The 5 days of protest that followed averaged over a thousand protestors. The protestors were angry and outraged against the way police had treated gays for decades. Although certainly not the first protest by gays, it was the most visible and explosive, starting the modern gay movement for equal rights and federal protection.

Today, every June cities around the USA hold festivals and parades. Equal rights, healthcare, and political agendas have been the primary platform, but unfortunately what the straight media exploits are the half naked party parade, cross dressers, and lesbians on motorcycles ("dykes on bikes"). The exception was the positive publicity of the AIDS Memorial Quilt in 1987 which focused attention on the lives lost to the HIV.

The Truth about HIV

Gays have long been associated with the "disease" AIDS (Acquired Immune Deficiency Syndrome), and for those who minutely still believe the causality fallacy, it is time to set the record straight. AIDS is not a plague sent by God to punish gays.[11] It is not a straight supremacist plot or conspiracy to intentionally kill gays. If anyone, politicians, law makers, public opinion, shear ignorance, and medical complacency are what and who I hold accountable for hundreds of thousands who have died inflicted with HIV (Human Immunodeficiency Virus, a virus that leads to the syndrome called AIDS).

When such sexually transmitted diseases like syphilis, gonorrhea and chlamydia scourged the straight promiscuous community, there was an outpour of concern and medical intervention, even when it was obvious these diseases were spread by unprotected sex, prostitution and wild philandering. Yet those in the promiscuous sect of the gay community were held in moral scrutiny by those screaming, "they brought it on themselves," and because of this double standard, so many people have unnecessarily died.

Adult consensual sex is not a crime and one should have nothing to be ashamed of or offer an apology for it. If a pathological agent endangers a community, any community, whether it spreads by airborne molecules or physical contact, the health care community has an obligation to isolate the contagion, and work toward education and eradication. When the CDC (Centers for Disease Control) established that there was an extremely serious crisis in the gay and Haitian refugee communities, the government withheld funding due to the fact that the crisis was affecting extremely unpopular communities. It was not until the virus emerged into the heterosexual IV drug using and hemophiliac community that it got a little more attention. Still, gays were stigmatized. Former president Ronald Reagan's submitted an apology in 1990 to be read at a Pediatric AIDS Foundation dinner for not giving the AIDS epidemic more attention,[12] The event confirmed the prejudicial attitudes which obscured the country's acknowledgement of the existence of the cross cultural AIDS epidemic and impeded efforts to obtain sufficient funding to fight the epidemic. That year, 1990, the House voted to provide the first significant amount of money, 4.5 billion dollars, for HIV testing and drug therapy.[13] At the end of 1990, 161,073 cases of AIDS had been reported and 100,813 people had died.

Evidenced by the CDC cluster study, the virus entered into the gay community by a Canadian flight attendant ("patient zero") who had sex with multiple male partners.[11] The gay community of the late 1970 to early 1980's sheltered many who embraced the behavior of having sex with many different consenting friends. The virus spread rapidly in the community as a result.

But let's not start there. That is not when, where and with whom HIV immerged. Situations and cultures that lend themselves to untested transfusions, prostitution, condom aversion, IV drug use, multi-partner sex, and international travel are ideal for transmitting diseases such as HIV with no predilection to the gay or straight lifestyle. HIV is not a gay virus. It is a virus spread by behavior.

The Human Immunodeficiency Virus is a virus, that left untreated, will lead to destruction of the immune system. This will ultimately lead to death from diseases that take advantage of a compromised immune system. As it related to sexual encounters, it spreads through the exchange of bodily fluids like semen, vaginal fluid, and blood with absolutely no preference to what gender one wishes to have sex with. If infected semen is ejaculated into the mouth of a man or woman, the virus may be transmitted (swallowing or not). If infected semen is ejaculated into the anus or vagina, the virus may be transmitted. If infected blood from a man or woman enters the urethra orifice of a man or a break in the skin of either a man or woman, the virus may be transmitted. If infected vaginal fluid enters the urethra orifice of a man, break in the skin, or makes contact with the oral mucosa of either a man or woman, the virus may be transmitted.[11] In straight or gay sex, HIV can be passed from one person to another.

As of 2006, pain staking research points to the origin of HIV being an almost identical virus carried by chimpanzees and other primates. It is unclear of how exactly this virus got into the human population, but some speculate(d) that it was probably through consumption of the meat, the butchering or skinning of the carcass, or the use of kidney cells to make a human vaccine.[14, 15] The first human cases have ties to the Cameroon and Congo regions of Africa.

Due to the fact that blood and tissue samples are kept on file at many clinics, researchers can actually go back and re-test suspicious patients for evidence of the virus; suspicious in the sense that they died from similar symptoms and syndromes we see today in AIDS patients. This was done on tissue and blood taken in 1959 from a man who, as far as investigators know, was heterosexual living in the Democratic Republic of Congo. HIV was found in his blood.

The same was found in the tissue of a British sailor who fell ill in 1957 and later died in 1959 from what was later found to be Pneumocystis Carinii Pneumonia (PCP). By all accounts, the man lived a heterosexual life being permitted to serve in the royal navy.[16] A heterosexual Norwegian sailor, his wife and his daughter too died of unusual circumstances between 1971–1976; all showing signs before death of drastic weight loss, skin sores, dementia and pneumonia. Their tissues were also contaminated with HIV. They lived for four years in Africa. In Europe, Africa, and in the U.S. there are many cases of documented peculiar deaths from similar symptoms and they are now being tested. Some cases have no tissues saved, so no definitive conclusions can be drawn from those.[17]

Who is to say where and by whom "patient zero," the fight attendant, got infected; probably another man, yes, and he from maybe another man, who slept with a bisexual married man, who got it from his wife, who secretly slept with exotic travelers, one of which who contracted the virus from a woman whose late husband died mysteriously in Kinshasa, Congo. That possible scenario is neither here or there, don't you see? The virus somehow crossed communities in the middle 70's from the straight community into the gay community, and if a virus, this virus, enters into a community that shares sexual partners, then the community as a whole is in danger; especially one that lives, works, plays, and congregates in concentrated numbers in specific locations; i.e. the Castro in San Francisco, or Greenwich and Fire Island in New York, refugee campus of South Florida.

When HIV became an epidemic in the gay community and followed soon-after in the Haitian refugee community, the U.S. government turned a blind eye, refused to recognize the epidemic as such, cast blame on the dieing victims, and provided limited funding and attention to combating the disease. Shame on them. Politicians call the delay in medical funding *red tape*. I say, "red tape, my ass". It was plain and simple homophobia and racism.

Now, in the U.S close to 600,000 souls are dead, succumbing to infection of AIDS, and 1.5 million are infected with HIV.[17] Needless to say, it was only a matter of time before it "**re-crossed** communities"; which it did in the late 80's to early 90s. Of the 600,000 dead, 200,000 are from heterosexual contact. The fastest *growing* population for HIV infections is the heterosexual youths. African Americans though comprise 52% of new cases in America. Gays are not at fault, as straights are not at fault for all the many disease in the past due to their natural behavior. Instead of trying to cast blame, blame that does nothing to help the problem only stigmatize a group, can we not work together to find a solution, to educate the young, to help the afflicted, and to learn from mistakes made?

In 1987, a beautiful show of support and compassion was seen in the presenting of a quilt on the National Mall in Washington D.C. The quilt at that time had 1,920 names. A year later the quilt appeared with 8,288 names and heartfelt sentiments.[18] Our community banded together to take care of their own since we were getting limited support from the government. Cure AIDS Now and Meals on Wheels were created. Brothers for Brothers was established as well. The lesbian community stepped-in, making home visits, cooking, cleaning, taking care of the victims' animals, offering companionship, and making hospital runs and monetary donation for food and medication. Community awareness was everywhere to be seen.

Once we were told what "it" was and how "it" was spread, flyers and pamphlets were distributed, town meetings held, bath houses closed, "rubber" bins with free prophylactics made available, contribution through wills made, and gay and gay friendly health care professionals established pro bono practices. We have been a resilient community to withstand the abuses and trials of the past. We are slowly emerging from the fire. At the price of keeping quiet and invisible, most of us in the past had taken a position of nonviolence and set up defensive walls to protect what little rights we had. It is now, in the 21st century, you see gays, lesbians and transgenders becoming proactive in their health care, taking more of an offensive legal position while still maintaining a nonviolent approach. We have had so much of our dignity chipped away, it is a miracle not all of us have gone insane.

The homosexual community as a whole has gone through the worst of the AIDS pandemic. There are still many living with HIV, those who are crossing the river at present, and those still making unhealthy choices. Bear backing is no longer viewed as hip; just simply dangerous. Even women are open to prophylactics when performing cunnilingus, and implements during sex are generally not shared anymore. What we are today is a veteran community of experience. Those of us who survived the 80's and 90's are teaching those coming of age. We smile when thinking of the days-of-old when physical love was for the taking and bodies intertwined in a mountain of pleasure. Those of us who are left often raise our glasses and tearfully toast our missed friends. Steven, Maurio, Carlos, Jim, Pedro, Tom, Ce-Ce, John, Paul, Jorge, not a day goes by that I do not think of you and the great times shared. I miss you all very much, my friends. To you all …

References

1. Aldrich, R. & Wotherspoon, G. (2001). *Who's Who in Gay and Lesbian History: From Antiquity to World War II, Vol. 1.* London: Routledge.

2. Aldrich, R. & Wotherspoon, G. (2001). *Who's Who in Gay and Lesbian History: From World War II to Present Day Vol. 2.* London: Routledge.

3. Lang, S. (1997). Various Kinds of Two-Spirit People: Gender Variance and Homosexuality in Native American Communities. In S.E. Jacobs, W. Thomas & S. Lang (Eds), *Two Spirit People: Native American Gender Identity, Spirituality, Sexuality and Spirituality* (pp 100-118). Urbana: Illini Books.

4. Hinsch, B. (1990). *Passions of the Cut Sleeve: The Male Homosexual Tradition in China.* Berkeley: University of California Press.

5. "Homosexuality in Japan". (2006, November 16) *Wikipedia.* [On-line] URL http://en.wikipedia.org/wiki/Homosexuality_in_Japan

6. "Timeline of LGBT History". (2006, November 15) *Wikipedia.* [On-line] URL http://en.wikipedia.org/wiki/Timeline_of_LGBT_history

7. Norton, M. (1997). *Founding Mothers and Fathers: Gendered Power and the Forming of American Society.* New York: First Vintage Books Edition.

8. Feinberg, L. (2005, February 17). 1950's: Lavender Scare. *Workers World.* [On-line] URL http://www.workers.org/2005/us/lgbtseries_0224/index.html

9. Carter, D. (2004). Stonewall: *The Riot That Sparked the Gay Revolution.* New York: St Martin's Press.

10. Clarke, G. (2000). *Get Happy: The Life of Judy Garland.* New York: Random House.

11. Stine, G. (2005). *AIDS Update 2005.* San Francisco: Benjamin Cummings.

12. Behrman, G. (2004) *The Invisible People: How the U.S. Has Slept Through the Global AIDS Pandemic, the Greatest Humanitarian Catastrophe of Ort Time.* New York: Free Press.

13. Stewart, R. (1990, June 14). House Votes to Provide $4.5 Billion in AIDS Legislation. *Los Angeles Times.* p. 24 Pt A

14. Bailes, E., et al. (2003). Hybrid Origin of SIV in Chimpanzees, *Science,* 300:1713.

15. Blancou, P., et al. (2001). Polio Vaccine Samples not Linked to AIDS. *Nature,* 410, 1045-1046

16. Zhu, T., Ho, D.D. (1995). Was HIV present in 1959? *Nature,* 374:503-4.

17. Jonassen, T, Stene-Johansen, K., Berg, E.S., Hungnes, O., Lindboe, C.F, Frøland, S.S, et al. (1997). Sequence analysis of HIV-1 group O from Norwegian patients infected in the 1960s. *Virology* 231:43-7.

18. History of the Quilt. (2006). *The AIDS Quilt Memorial.* [Online] URL http://www.aidsquilt.org/history.htm

10

Subcultures and Symbols

The term "homosexuality" is said to have been first coined and used around 1838 in describing people having sexual attraction and/or relationships with that of the same sex.[1] It appeared in American medical journals in 1890 and was in common use by 1920. *Homo* means same and *sexuality* is self explanatory. As mentioned in chapter 4 the term worked its way into the DSM in 1952 as a mental illness later to be removed in 1973. In the middle of the twentieth century there was a movement in the community for the replacement of the term *homosexual* with *homophilic* emphasizing the love aspect of the relationship rather than the sex.[2] The movement was unfortunately short lived.

The term *gay* is an adjective meaning happy and carefree. It was used without prejudice in film, radio, literature, and on the street well into the 20th century to describe unmarried "straights" uninhibited by moral constraints. For example, there was a book and later a film called The Gay Falcon (1941) which was about a womanizing male detective.[3] A few years before, Cary Grant used it in Bringing Up Baby (1938) when, because his clothes had been sent to the cleaners, he was jeered when seen wearing a lady's feathery robe. "Come on fellows, it's not like I just suddenly turned gay all of a sudden." It is said that "gay" meant *flashy, girly, un-manly* to most movie goers; not necessarily homosexual. Mr. Grant's, later to come out of the closet, was quoted in saying, "I knew the connotation of the term, even if the audience did not." *Gay* was ad-libbed. It wasn't written in the script.[4] The connotations of flashy and showiness in dress ("gay attire") led to association with pretty and girly, and then to its current dominant meaning, which was at first confined to subcultures. The subcultural usage started to become mainstream in the 1960s, when *gay* became the term predominantly preferred by homosexual men to describe themselves. *Gay* was the preferred term since other terms, such as "queer" and "faggot" were felt to be derogatory. "Homosexual" was perceived as excessively clinical: especially since homosexuality was at that time designated as a mental illness.

Queer has traditionally meant strange, unusual, weird, and rare. It was seen peppered in stories such as the 1914 The Dark Flower, "The tree growth there was too thick—the queer stumps and snags had uncanny shapes, as if monstrous creatures, where eyes seemed to peer out at you".[5] The behavior of homosexuals was viewed as strange and unusual, even weird so the name fit the characteristics observed by straights, and soon the term used to labeled the individuals. Starting around the 1950's, *queer* was viewed as a derogatory term for homosexuals but now, as a new immergence in the community, the term is used freely as a term that encompasses gays, lesbians, bisexuals, intersex, and transgenders. Pridefully, we embrace the fact that we *are* unusual in the secular world.

Unlike queer, *faggot,* is still extremely derogatory. Its etymology leads us back to medieval England where "faggots" were bundles of sticks used for burning. As a matter of fact, a fag in British English still refers to a cigarette, and the un-smoked end called the fag-end. Linguistic evidence points to outcast witches, who were burned with the sticks/stakes, being called faggots. Old British literature refers to old unpleasant women as faggots; maybe a literary descendent of the witches. In the early 1900's extremely feminine men were taunted as "acting like funny old women" and soon the faggot work its way into the vocabulary.[6] The earliest known homosexual reference to the word in print was in *A Vocabulary of Criminal Slang, with Some Example of Common Usage* by Louis Jackson (1914), "All the faggots will be dressed in drag at the ball tonight." [7]

The word *lesbian* is derived from Lesbos, a Greek island located in the Aegean Sea. According to Greek mythology the island was inhabited by the Amazons, an entirely female warrior nations. Males inhabited the island as well but they apparently were used as sperm contributors and in a support role to the warriors. The protection of the island was not dependent on the men, and the women held the political and social upper hand. However, that is just myth. The true etymology of *lesbian* stems from a Greek lyric poet by the name of Sappho. Sappho was born between 630 BC and 612 BC in Eresos on the Greek island of Lesbos. Her poems spoke of love for men and infatuations for women. But put in context of the time, her homoerotica poems were extremely controversial.[8] Her infatuations on the island were directed towards the women of Lesbos, or the *beautiful Lesbians.* Eventually, the term evolved into a derogatory term for women who engaged in homoerotica activities. Today, female homosexuals are frequently referred to, without derogatory connotation, as lesbians to distinguish from male homosexuals. So when a distinction needs to be made, gay is reserved for males and lesbians for females. Most females on the other hand have limited qualms with the label of gay. Most men though may take umbrage in being called lesbian.

Within the gay and lesbian community, there are subcultures and colorful terms and labels. Let me preface this section by stressing that not all queers subscribe to these labels or any labels at all, but since they do exist in the community I thought it may warrant mention. On the male side, there are those who wish to be associated as tops (or pitchers), the active partner in anal sex, and bottoms (or catchers), those who are penetrated during anal sex. One does not necessarily have to be one or the other. Then there are the Bears and the Cubs; where Bears are gay men (usually a little on the heavy-side) noted by the excessive body and facial hair, and the Cubs are smaller younger often submissive men who enjoys the company of Bears.[9] On the ladies side, we have lots of fun categories such as luppies, lipstick lesbians, femmes, chapstick lesbians, granola lesbians, butch and bulldykes. The luppies are the urban professional lesbians. The lipstick lesbians have glamorous feminine characteristics and who are usually attracted to other feminine women. The femmes also have glamorous feminine characteristics but tend to be drawn toward the more masculine lesbians. The butch lesbians embrace a more masculine appearance, with attributes, and behaviors coinciding like deliberate chivalry. The bulldyke has adopted a very masculine appearance, aggressive-machismo in behavior and are often, without insult, mistaken for men. The chapstick lesbian also called the G.Q. lesbian has a more handsome androgynous appearance and usually is the athletic types. The granola lesbians are those who embrace nutritional health, spiritual health and natural states of existence rather subscribing to superficial outward appearances.[9]

Just as there were secret places to gather due to the non acceptance of our lifestyle, there were (still are) secret indicators to signal that you were of a gay persuasion. It made identifying each other more efficient without encroaching, intruding, or making a very costly mistake of approaching non-receptive heterosexual. The red handkerchief was a gay indicator back in the days when men wore them in the front pocket of a blazer. Then there was, once you had caught the eye of someone, to look from shoes to knees, back to the shoes and then slowly looking away in the direction of travel, signaling "follow me so we can talk". The right ear piercing or right lone earring in the 70's and 80s became a popular indicator of gayness. Today, identifying each other out in a crowd is becoming increasingly challenging. Most of us just wait until a platonic conversation leads into who they are dating or just broke up with, and wait for a pronoun or lack of one to be used.

Symbols and Flags

The rainbow flag is by far the most recognizable symbol of gay pride today in United States. There is a rich history behind this flag. During the Peasant War in Germany 1524–1525, a rainbow flag was flown by the peasants as a sign of a new era, or hope and of social change. Again we see a rainbow flag immerging in Italy in 1961 used in a peace march. The colors starting from the top were blue, turquoise, purple, green, yellow, orange and red. In 1978, at the Gay Freedom Day

Parade in San Francisco California, a rainbow flag, hand dyed by Gilbert Baker and flown by Justin Fox, ushering in a new era of gay symbols. The original gay pride rainbow flag had eight colors rather than the six you see today. From top to bottom the colors were hot pink—sexuality, red-life, orange-healing, yellow-sunlight, green-nature, turquoise-magic, blue-serenity and violet-spirit. When demand for the flags exploded exponentially that year and into 1979, the hot pink stripe was dropped due to the unavailability of the hot pink fabric. The flag then became 7 stripes. A few months before the turn of the decade, flags were seen hanging from the lamp posts on Market Street in San Francisco. They were hung vertically with the post directly in the middle of the draped flag. The center stripe was obscured by the post due to the odd numbered, 7, total stripes in the flag; (3 colors on one side 3 colors on the another and one obscured color in the middle). To remedy this, one more color was dropped making the flag 6 colors. Today the rainbow flag is red, orange, yellow, green, blue, and violet. Although gay pride is the central theme, it also symbolizes the original meaning of hope, social change and a sign of a new era.[10]

The pink and black triangles, as the rainbow flag, are very popular symbols (the pink more so than the black) in the gay community. In the 1930's in Nazi Germany, homosexuals were arrested and incarcerated along with the Jews, Poles, Communists Gypsies, and "anti-socials". At the concentration camps, each prisoner had to wear some form of a triangle to designate what he or she was incarcerated for. The Jews wore two yellow triangles overlapping to form the Star of David. Regular prisoners wore a green triangle. The anti-socials like prostitutes, women who refuse to bear children, and lesbians were forced to wear a black triangle. Gay men wore the pink triangle. Wearing the pink triangle disproportionately exposed the inmates to excessive abuse from guards and other inmates.[11, 12] As addressed in Chapter 2, approximately 60,000 homosexuals were killed under the Nazi regime. What most do not know is that after the liberations of the prison and concentration camp survivors in 1945, the Jews, Serbs, Gypsies, Communists, and Poles were released while the homosexuals remained prisoners for decades because of a 1935 version of a law called Paragraph 175 remained law in West Germany. This was, as many, another ugly scar in history.[12]

Paragraph 175

§ 175 Lewdness (anal sex) between men

I. A man who engages as the active or passive partner in lewdness with another man is to be punished by imprisonment.

II. With an involved party who at the time of the act had not yet reached the age of twenty-one years, the Court can refrain from punishment in mild cases.

> *§ 175a Severe lewdness (Schwere Unzucht)*
> A punishment of up to ten years in the penitentiary, and even with mitigating circumstances no less than three months imprisonment for:
>
> 1. a man, who by force or by threat of harm to life and limb forces another man to engage in such an act as either the active or passive partner;
>
> 2. a man, who by abusing a dependency founded in a service-, work-, or employment-based relationship coerces another man into engaging in such an act as either the active or passive partner;
>
> 3. a man over twenty-one years old who entices a male under twenty-one years old to engage in such an act as either the active or passive partner;
>
> 4. a man who professionally offers himself for such an act as either the active or passive partner.

The lambda sign (λ) was adopted in 1970 by New York Gay Activists Alliance and in 1974 it was adopted by the International Gay Rights Congress. It is a symbol of lesbian and gay rights. It is not clear though what the lambda actually symbolizes. Some hold on to the use in physics where lambda denotes energy or synergy, where the whole is greater than the sum of it parts. Some hold on to the Greek lower case letter for "l" meaning liberation, or some believe in the Roman meaning of lambda, "light of knowledge shed into the darkness of ignorance." The lambda sign is more internationally recognizable than the rainbow flag.[10]

The organization called the Human Rights Campaign (HRC) also has a distinctive flag. The background in a royal blue and two parallel horizontal yellow/gold bars signifying equality. HRC founded in 1980 is an advocacy group for lesbians, gays, bisexuals transsexuals and transgenders. They strive for equal rights and safe communities by educating the public on various issues, legislations and laws, and by keeping a scorecard on those in office and those running for public office. In sporting their logo, many gays and non gays (gay allies) are publicizing their support of what the organization stands. I highly recommend HRCs web site www.hrc.org for a variety of links, taking action strategies, and the latest in the struggle for equal recognition. In the next chapter I will go more in depth on the resources available.

There is an ever growing sense of pride in the community where people are flying their rainbow, pink triangle or lambda flags, wearing their pride pins or displaying pride bumper stickers. Now, I know some straights may be asking, "why do they do that? You don't see us publicizing that we are straight." First of all, that position is not a legitimate question of inquiry; it is a not-so-subtle attack with a "we don't do it, so you shouldn't either" attitude. The response to that type of reasoning is that "straights" were never made to hide the fact they were straight.

So until you have walked in the shoes of forced secrecy, public humiliation and societal banishment, you have absolutely no grounds to belittle or condemn the action of our newly found confidence. We no longer have to live in as much fear as we were forced to endure for generations. Sporting our pride paraphernalia is a bold and liberating, symbolic proclamation. It screams to those who take notice that we exist, that we are no longer hiding, and instead of continuing to be made to feel less than human, we are a proud people. Some liberal heterosexuals sport the bumper stickers and flags as well in solidarity. They are saying through symbol that they are aware of our plight and they support change for a just and equitable society. Eventually, and I hope in my lifetime, there would be no cause to advertise one's sexual orientation. But until we are treated as equals in our own right, not subjected to social indignity, not victimized and where sexual orientation is inconsequential, we will force the issue that we are here to stay. Until I can matter-of-factly say, "Yes, I am gay" and that statement be received without issue as, "Yes, I am straight", we will march on. You do not need to participate in our lifestyle, as we wish not to join or succumb to your sexual ways of life. We all, homosexual, heterosexuals, bisexuals, transgenders, and transsexuals, need to merely co-exist equally and peacefully together. There is room for all. Just give peace and respect a chance.

116   Why We March

References

1. Feray, Jean-Claude and Herzer, Manfred, trans. Glen W. Pepple, (1990). Homosexual Studies and Politics in the 19th Century: Karl Maria Kertbeny. *Journal of Homosexuality* Vol. 19 no. 1.

2. "Homophile" (2006, November 10) *Wikipedia*. [On-line] URL: http://en.wikipedia. org/wiki/Homophile_Movement

3. Arlen, M. (1941). The Gay Falcon. *Town & Country*. Vol 5.

4. Russo, V. (1987). *The Celluloid Closet: Homosexuality in the Movies*. Harrow & Row.

5. Galsworthy, J. (1914). *The Dark Flower*. New York: Scribner's Son.

6. "Faggot". (1994). *Random House Historical Dictionary of American Slang*. In J.E. Lighter (Ed). New York: Random House.

7. Jackson, L (1914). *A Vocabulary of Criminal Slang with Some examples of Common Usage*. Williston Modern Printing Company.

8. Hubbard, T. (2003). *Homosexuality in Greece & Rome: A Sourcebook of Basic Documents*. Berkeley: University of California Press.

9. "Queer Slang in the Gay 90s." (1993). *Alyson Almanac 1994–1995 Edition: The Fact Book of the Lesbian and Gay Community*. Alyson Publication. [On-line] URL: www. gaymart.com

10. Haggerty, G. (2000). *Gay Histories and Cultures*. New York: Garland Publishing Inc.

11. Dynes, W., Donaldson, S., Johansson, W.; Percy, W. (1990). *The Encyclopedia of Homosexuality*. New York: Garland Publishing Inc.

12. Heger, H., Muller, K., Fernbach, D., (1980). *The Men with the Pink Triangle: The True Life and Death Story of Homosexuals in the Nazi Death Campus*. London: Gay Men's Press.

11

Where From Here

Besides beating the drum and carrying the lead sign in the next gay parade, there is much you can do to support equality. By taking little baby steps you will build confidence in where you stand on the issues at hand. There is no getting around the fact that homosexuality is not very popular. It is controversial. It is attacked, ridiculed and even vilified in the news, in churches, around the dining room table, in locker rooms and in office cubicles. Please understand this one truth. Homosexuality is not wrong. Many people, as those you will encounter, embrace the predictability of life so they fear what they do not understand. Some latch on to public opinion before their own opinion can be shaped with the true reality.

First things first. You have to get used to homosexuals being in your life. Also you have get use to gay implacable words. These two words, *gay* and *lover*, seem to get the best of the budding-gay friendly people into a linguistical panic. You, as an empathetic heterosexual, need to say and get use to the word "gay." Say *gay* out loud so you hear your own voice. Say it enough times that you no longer knit your brow when it is said. Use it in a sentence. For example, "My son/daughter/secretary/teacher is gay" then personalize the noun with a name, "Sam is gay." Say it once, think through what you said and say it again putting emphasis on a different word each time. When you have grown use to hearing and saying "gay" to yourself, graduate to saying it to an inanimate object like a picture of someone you care about. "Sam is gay. Sam is gay, Sam is gay." The same goes for the word *lover*. "Sam's lover is Josh. Josh is Sam's lover."

Now, some gays and lesbians do not appreciate their partners being referred to as lovers because it overemphasizes the sex and minimizes the oneness of mind and soul. Others really do not care. If you are unsure of what to say, go with *partner*. That is safe. Once a name has been worked into the conversation you may ask, "Sam, are you ok with me referring to Josh as your lover?"

If your gay friend or family member just started seeing someone, lover or partner would not be appropriate. Try *girlfriend* or *boyfriend*. Start using pronouns whenever you can. This minor expression acknowledges the fact that you understand and are aware of the fact that they are gay. When all else fail, just ask your-self what would feel comfortable to you if the tables were turned.

Issues

I was in a meeting several years back and I heard an insensitive colleague say, "Students, after tuition is paid, like to Jew their money. So forget about asking them for lab fees." After what he said sank in, I politely interjected and expressed first my disappointment in hearing such anti-Semitic words leave his lips, and then I told him that I would not be party to a meeting or organization that disrespects Jews or any other group. I was not trying to be overly noble, but disrespect is what it is. I was not looking for approval from those who were present. What was said was rude. Did it put my Catholicism into question? No!! Am I Jewish? No, I am not, and I do not need to be to support human rights issues. Either do you.

Supporting gay issues and fighting for equal rights should not put anyone's sexuality in question. Many still feel it does. "If I voice support or object to off-colored jokes, people may think I am queer. If they do, I will be ostracized and looked upon with suspicion. I may lose my job, never get a date, get teased, or maybe get assaulted." Welcome to our world. Are you getting the point of why we march? Homosexuality is so unpopular or so misunderstood that many, although supportive, still distance themselves from us and issues concerning the basic humanity. I would like to think about this phenomenon like an empty dance floor. The music is inviting and you know many want to dance. You see them swaying or bobbing in their chairs or by the bar. The problem is that no one is on the dance floor yet. You do not want to be the first because you do not want to be stared at. Unfortunately, a good number of patrons are thinking the same. One brave person or a couple of people step upon the floor and eventually people gravitate to the floor. What I am saying is, DO THE RIGHT THING. Support human rights. You are not alone. You'll see there are more of you out there.

For successful implementation of human rights legislation, we need the support of all those who believe in human rights issues. Bills, court orders and legislation are being killed in Congress and at State Committee hearings due to conserva-tive homo-hatists presenting them in a negative, inaccurate, unsubstantiated light based on their fears and prejudices. They are proactive in the quest to perpetuate hatred and to blatantly deny us social integration. If more people do not come forward to present the issue in the true reality, then all the committee hears are the lies and biases. We, gays, lesbians, bisexuals and transgenders cannot gener-ate the numbers and the votes by ourselves. We need support from all those who believe in equality and justice. Too many bills are being killed or tabled due to complacency. And there are some who believe that by not voting against us, they are supporting us. Although much appreciated, it is not enough.

What many do not realize is that all our (straight and gay) protection rights, access rights, exclusions, inclusion, the can-dos and can't dos, all reverberate from laws, regulations and policies; not a conscience of love and respect for each other as we may like. If the written law can be interpreted to exclude a certain group, then a new law has to be written to include that group, or that group will be legally excluded. A case in point was the right to vote. It was interpreted and upheld that it included only white men. So laws had to be drawn to include women and then all races including blacks. One can discriminate against a group if the law doesn't specifically include that group. Discrimination can take all forms; housing, schools, access to private or public property, transportation etc. Attorneys actually go into the courtroom and argue, "where does it say that one has to allow those people into your building or where does it say that they should be privy to this benefit?" If the answer is, "It doesn't say it anywhere," then the person in question cannot enjoy the life, liberty, and the pursuit of happiness as others do. There are the new laws authored by bigots that actually specifically read that gays cannot this and aren't allowed to do that or are "banned". A case in point is the right to adopt. It defines this social human right as exclusively open to a certain group: heterosexuals. Marriage, for example, is in certain states defined as between one man and one woman instead of marriage being defined as a life long commitment rooted in love between consenting non-related adults.[1] Another one of many laws of exclusion is pension benefits of the deceased to be forwarded to the surviving spouse as defined through legal civil marriage.[2] Since we cannot marry, or have a union recognized as marriage by the federal government, our partners are not privy to the pension benefits.

If we cannot drum up the numbers to defeat such bills, they may become law. Complacency and indifference from our allies is hurting us more than ever.

Some policies and laws are on a state level, others are on a federal level. The legislative process is a long systematic process, but for those who are steadfast, informed and proactive, they can change the rules by which we live. It is oh so common to hear someone say, "How the heck did that become law?" The answer is that the bill in question may have been introduced by a bigoted law maker, presented in a negative light, then left unchallenged by those unaware it was being voted on at the committee hearing or on the floor of the legislative house; by those assuming that goodness and respect will always win out in the end, or by those who think someone else will challenge the gay repressive proposed bill. The same goes for bills needing support. If the hetero-supremists are aggressively presenting their vile objections to the bill and a limited amount of people are expressing their support, once again assuming that a just and righteous bill will win on it own merit without proactive support, the bill will die.

A case in point: in Florida a series of Bills were introduced to remove the ban on homosexuals adopting. It would define the standards as in the best interest of the person to be adopted and require an assessment of prospective parents. Florida Senate Committee on Children was scheduled to vote on this bill on February 14, 2006. The vote was postponed due to lack of support and then died when legislature adjourned on May 5, 2006. So as things stand in Florida, homosexuals are banned from adopting children; yet single men and women can adopt (refuting the argument that a stable home needs both a Mom and Dad) and convicted felons can adopt.[3, 4] We could provide a safe, loving, stable home to a child or children in foster care; yet we are banned because of what; fear that we may damage the child, hurt the child, convert the child, or influence the child? What is our crime? Our lifestyle has no influence on what sexual orientation will manifest itself in the child. Our influence on a heterosexual child is about as powerful as our heterosexual parent had on us. Homosexuality, heterosexuality, bisexuality are innate. A parent cannot convert a child one way or the other.[5] According to the American Psychological Association and many research studies, "There is no scientific basis for concluding that lesbian mothers or gay fathers are unfit parents on the basis of their sexual orientation."[6, 7] An abusive parent, though, can force a lifestyle unnatural to the child on the child, but the members of the Florida assembly are assuming that we are or will be abusive. The members of the assembly are being brainwashed in thinking that we are, or that not enough people are fighting to let them know we are, can be, and will be great parents.

Allow me to digress a bit and address the legislative process. This is how an idea becomes a state law. There are three branches to government; legislative, executive and judicial. The legislative branch has the exclusive law making power. Most states have two houses in the legislative branch. States like Maryland have a Senate and a House of Delegates together called the General Assembly. In California, the houses are called the Senate and the Assembly. In Florida the two houses are called the Senate and the House of Representative. Whatever the designation, most of our states have two houses in their legislative branch of government. Few states like Nebraska only have a Senate house in the Legislature, having only 49 members. In Maryland there are 42 senators and 141 delegates. In Florida, there are 40 senators and 120 members of the House of Representatives. Every state has a different number. A concerned or misguided citizen or group convinces a member of the legislative branch of the state government to introduce, support and champion an idea. This member of either one of these houses submits the formally written idea to Legislative Counsel where it is drafted into a Bill format, and read on the floor of whatever the house the representative belongs. At this point it is given a number and sent to a particular committee made up of a certain number from each house for debate.

Now, there are many committees. For example, there is an Insurance Committee, a Senate Health and Human Services Committee, a Criminal Justice Committee, a Committee on Children and Families, etc. The Bill is assigned to the Committee that handles such issues. At the committee hearing, the author introduces the bill, and members hear testimonies and discuss various points of view. It is voted on by approving, defeating or amending. If the committee votes to approve the Bill, it is read, discussed and voted-on again but this time on the floor in the House it originated. Once a bill has been approved by the house from which it originated, it is sent to the other house. For example, if it was approved by the state senate, it then goes to the House of Delegates (Maryland). Once both houses approve the bill, it goes to the Governor. The governor of the state can perform three actions, 1) sign it into law, 2) allow it to become law without a signature, or 3) veto it. It usually takes 2/3 majority vote by both houses to override a veto.

It would be political suicide for an elected official to vote contrary to the perceived consensus of his/her constituents. Most representatives and senators actually vote based on the limitation of their experience with the issue. If all they are hearing are negatives, attacks, filth, and foul, then of course they will not support any issues concerning gay inclusion. Even an open minded official may not vote based on his/her kind conscience, because that which is obviously the right thing to do may not be the most popular move to make. If there are no opposing views, they may base their vote on who is screaming the loudest and, goodness gracious, are those Christian Conservatives loud. This is why it is imperative to inform your elected officials that you are one of many who are against discrimination and violence motivated by intolerance, and that you are in support of them doing the right thing in fighting prejudice.

If sexual orientation is not included in an existing anti-discrimination state law, then it is legal to deny gays, lesbians, or transgenders employment for example. General antidiscrimination exclusion will allow employment terminated based solely on sexual orientation, deny entrance to schools, deny credit, and deny housing or acceptance from a condo association. In Iowa, a bill was introduced that would add sexual orientation and gender identity to the state law prohibiting discrimination in employment, public accommodation, education, real estate transactions, and credit. It was rejected on May 3, 2006. Shame on Iowa, and shame on the other 24 states that allow discrimination.[8] Shame on you if you don't support a bill in your state that prohibits discrimination!

If sexual orientation and gender identity is not included in public and private schools harassment and bullying policy, then those that that are guilty of harassing or bullying a child based on that premise may not be punished in accordance with the standard reprimand. Yes, there is punishment for hitting or harassing another child, but similar to the state's Hate Crime laws, if the harassment is based on hate toward an identifiable group, then harsher punishments may be warranted. At present most schools have a written policy prohibiting inappropriate behavior targeting children and teachers based on many identifiable characteristics ... but not sexual orientation. It is a huge concern at the junior high and high school level where children are becoming aware of where their attractions naturally lie. In Iowa and Florida a series of bills were introduced requiring local school districts and accredited private schools to adopt policies that included sexual orientation and gender identity as one the many categories of protection from intimidation, harassment, and bullying. The categories of protection already established are religion, race, color, national origin, age, sex, disability, height, weight, and socioeconomic status. The bill was defeated in Iowa on May 3, 2006 and in Florida on May 5, 2006. Shame on Iowa, Florida, and other states that reject this inclusion! Support a bill in your state that includes sexual orientation and gender identity as a part of school bullying and harassment policy.[9, 10]

If the federal government and states do not include sexual orientation and gender identity in their Hate Crime law, less severe sentences and retribution would be imposed on those found guilty; setting a precedent that crimes against the GLBT community are not as serious and extensive as those committed against the groups already included. Crimes against homosexuals and transgenders far outnumber crimes based on sex, national origin, and religion (those characteristics being included in hate crime law). While five states do not have any specific laws that address hate or bias crimes, thirteen states have hate laws and are insistent on excluding sexual orientation or gender identity. These states include Alabama, Alaska, Idaho, Michigan Mississippi, Montana, North Carolina North Dakota, Ohio, Oklahoma, South Dakota, Virginia, and West Virginia.[11, 12] Support bills and initiatives in your state that seek to add sexual orientation and gender identity to the hate crime law or support the creation of a hate crimes policy, inclusive of all vulnerable and victimized groups.

When a homosexual couple makes a life long commitment with each other, obligations and responsibility come with that commitment. First and most importantly, we love each other and wish to be together, even if confined to a nursing home. As things stand, we can be forced apart due to the unmarried status.[13] If children have been introduced into the family, then the non paternal or non maternal partner must have a legal bond to the child in order to make medical and educational decisions and must have custody if the biological parent dies. To merely pick up a child from the school office requires a family member.

If a legal spousal bond does not exist, there is no family. A spouse is the most important person in the other's life. Two lives become one; financially in filing taxes, in bank accounts, in property ownership, etc. We should be able to share these privileges. We should not be compelled or subpoenaed to testify against each other. Because our life partners are not recognized under federal law as family, at present we cannot take advantage of the Family and Medical Leave Act that permit leave to care for them if seriously ill or hospitalized. We must be granted inclusion. If incarcerated, one should be allowed conjugal visitation from the other. Current U.S. immigration law does not allow lesbian, gay or bisexual citizens or permanent residents to petition for their same-sex partners to immigrate.[14] If medical decisions need to be made, we should be able to make them for the other as well as see each other if hospitalized. If one dies without a will, inheritance should be given to the other partner.

We should be allowed to reap compensation for wrongful death or receive federal assistance if another tragedy like September 11, 2001 occurs. The surviving partner should be allowed bereavement leave. As things stand today, we are not.[15] If relocating or traveling through another state, the legal union between the two should be recognized. All of what is listed above are only available it we have the right to marry. It hurts no one to extend these rights to us. We are people just like you who fell in love. You, as an ally, must oppose bills and initiatives that define legal marriage as being between a man and a woman. The law would legally exclude us for any marital rights.

If you are still fighting internally with the religious or the biblical morality of marriage, then support a bill, like the one introduced in Rhode Island, that allows same sex couple to marry in accordance with state law, and clarifies that religious institutions and clergy would not be compelled to perform these marriages.[16] The church need not recognize it. If still on the fence concerning supporting same sex marriage, then for goodness sakes support domestic partnership or civil union inclusion bills. Yes, these bills give less recognition than a marriage, because the civil unions and domestic partnership may not be recognized in another state as well as have no Federal recognition, but at least it is a step in the right direction instead of keeping the disgraceful situation the way it is today.

The present situation as of Fall 2006 is that only Massachusetts has legalized gay marriage, 3 states (Connecticut, New Jersey, and Vermont) provide state level spousal rights to same sex couples within their state, 1 state (California) provides almost all of the state level spousal rights to unmarried gay and straight couples who register as domestic partners, and 2 states (Hawaii, and Maine) and the District of Columbia have statewide laws that provide some spousal-like rights to unmarried gay and straight couples.[17] Most states already have domestic partnership laws but have chosen to exclude gays and lesbians. On a side note, for everyone registering as domestic partner an affidavit needs to be signed and notarized affirming that, 1) the intent for partnership is permanent, 2) neither are married to any individual, 3) both are 18 years of age or older, 4) both do not have a blood relation, 5) both are financially interdependent such that they are jointly responsible for the common welfare of the household, and 6) that they have been living in a committed exclusive relationship at least for an extended period of time (time varies from state to state). Therefore, not just any couple can take advantage of the domestic partnership law. It is a commitment no matter how you look at it.

The majority of the American states either have a State constitution or state laws restricting marriage to one man and one woman. We feel that if we love and support each other, are adults and unrelated, are sexually and emotionally exclusive, and desire to spend the rest of our lives with each other, we should be able to marry. Write your elected officials and express that you are against amending the state constitution on restricting marriage. Write your elected officials and express that you are in support of inclusion of gay and lesbian couples in the legal right of marriage. Support a bill and/or sign petitions supporting domestic partnership and civil union spousal rights for gay couples. For those still on the fence, you need to get past the visual "weirdness" of two tuxedoed grooms or two flowing white dresses at the alter, and focus on the lives of these two people who love each other. Let's stand together for what is just.

Napoleon Bonaparte, a general in the French Revolution, Emperor of France and King of Italy was quoted as saying, "Ten people who speak make more noise than ten thousand who are silent." We need our allies to step up and speak. Every citizen has the right to write to or seek a lobby visit with members of Congress or their elected state officials. Only 10% of Americans over a lifetime ever seek to contact members of their state or federal government. Below is a step by step way by which you can let your voice be heard.[18]

First though, you need to know what bills have been introduced, what the status of the bills is, what committee it has been assigned to, who is on the committee, and then the contact information of the committee members and committee chair. Depending on where the bill is in the legislative process, you may need to contact members of that house not just the committee members. In making your initial search for related bills, I do not suggest going directly to your state's website www.<state>.gov because there are thousands of bills to rifle through. The web site I love is www.hrc.org. They have a wealth of information on gay rights and focuses on legislation in each state pertinent to gays, lesbians and transgenders. Once on their home page, select "Take Action", then "Laws and Legislation in Your State". Select the state you are inquiring about. At this point you can choose "View Current Laws or View Current Legislation". Note and jot down the number at the top of the bill you are interested in, and read the full text of the bill so you are fully educated in specifics of the bill, who it affects, what the clauses are if any, and what committee the bill was assigned to. At this point, you can resort to your state government web site, www.<state>.gov and select the link that directs you to the state legislature. On most, if not all, government web sites, they will post who sits on what committee, their session and interim contact information. Now it is time to draft a letter or request a personal visit.

Personal visits are extremely effective when driving home certain issues. Your officials are people too. They are not as unapproachable as you may think. You can ask your elected official to explain their views and maybe even correct them on some inaccuracy on which they may be building their vote or opinion. For those who want to influence officials through a personal visit, this is the route to take.

Using the fax number available, send a meeting request letter:

Date

The Honorable _____
Full Address

Dear Senator/Representative _____:

I am writing to request the opportunity to meet with you to discuss bill # _____, sponsored by _____. It reads, <Quote the section(s) of the bill of concern>

< Write why it is of concern to you>

I am available during the next legislative recess. I will contact your office in the next few days to verify receipt of my request and to schedule a meeting. Thank you in advance for your time and willingness to communicate with your constituents.

Respectfully,
<sign>

Print or type name
Home Address (Email address)
Phone Number

In a few days (between 4–7 days), using the phone number available, call the office and ask to speak with the official's scheduler. Once the scheduler is on the line explain that you are a constituent who wishes to schedule a visit with the official to discuss the specific bill. Let the scheduler know the bill number and the name of the bill. Also mention that you faxed written request a few days prior. On the date and time given arrive a little early, dress in business attire, and bring a note pad and pen. Introduce yourself and always address the official by his/her title. Shake hands, be polite, sit up straight, and most importantly thank them for seeing you. Stay away from the chit chat because the official has a busy schedule. Smile whenever possible to cut the tension. Remember they are on edge also, expecting to be put on the defensive. Get to the point of what bill you would like to discuss, how you feel and why. Then ask them where they stand on the issue and why. Take notes and wait for them to finish. Address first the points, if any, that you agree with and that coincides with your position. Then address point by point where you both disagree and why. Try not to get too emotional, loud or informal. Never use foul language. Instead of, "That's such Bullshit!" try, "What evidence supports your claim?" Do not feel defeated if you cannot come to an agreement. Most officials come away from these types of meetings with another perspective; especially if the person facing them is one of them, "straight".

Option two is to write a letter. Again, both in-session and out-of-session addresses and phone numbers for state senators and representatives are on the state government's website. I have heard that a handwritten letter has more of a chance of being read, so handwrite your letter; even the envelope. Since it is in hand script, make an asserted effort to write legibly. My humble suggestion, since we have all gotten use to spell check and grammar check, is to type the letter out first, spell check it, then copy it in your handwriting. Remember that most state legislatures are in session the first part of the year, so if in session, address it to their state capital office and when out of session address the letter to the local district office.

Your Name
Your Address
Your Phone Number
Email address

Date
The Honorable _____
State House (Room Number)
Full Address
Dear Senator/Representative _____:

*   Identify the bill by the bill number and describe it by popular title
*   Write your own views—not someone else's
*   Give your reasons for taking a stand; not statements like "Vote against S 2.3.4.; I am bitterly opposed." but rather, for example. "I am a high school teacher is upper Florida and I see many gay students being harassed on a weekly basis with little being done to the bullies guilty of such damaging behavior ..."
*   Be factual not emotional

---

* If against a bill, be constructive and write what would make it right
* If an expert in the subject the bill is targeting, express your credentials
* Keep your letter to one page
* Do not make threats. That may get you a visit from the Secret Service, NO JOKE!!
* Do not berate the representative
* Do not pretend to wield vast political influence
* Thank the member for taking the time to read your letter
* Never demand a response

Respectfully,
<sign>
Print or type name

Perhaps the most important lesson to take away from this book is that gays, lesbians, bisexuals, and trangenders are living breathing souls with needs, feelings, wants, desires, contributions, vulnerability, and achievements, and are deserving of respect and inclusion. Taken as a whole, we are a people filled with goodness, geneosity, love, and so much to offer society. We have been an integral part of shaping America. When we raise our voice to sing "America the Beautiful" remember that the author of the poem from which the lyrics came was written by a lesbian by the name of Katherine Lee Bates (1859–1929). She and her life partner Katherine Coman were together for 25 years before Ms. Coman died of cancer in 1915.[19]

We have fought in the wars of past and fighting in the wars at present. We protect the streets on which you walk. We teach the schools you attend. We are your doctors and nurses, decorators and plumbers, artists and playwrights, and we have brought home the gold while you cheered with American pride. We were the trail blazers for women athletics and broke down the barriers of gender-type jobs. There is no doubt we exist and pose no more a threat than heterosexuals. It is time for us to come out of the shadows of secrecy and live safe, honest, wholesome lives. Our intimate lifestyle may be different from yours but not to be seen as wrong. If you haven't already, get to know us. You'll see there is nothing to fear. And maybe, just maybe, you'll march with us.

References

1. National Conference of State Legislatures (2006). *Same Sex Marriage.* URL [On-line] http://www.ncsl.org/programs/cyf/samesex.htm

2. Curry, H., Clifford, D., Hertz, F. (2205). *A Legal Guide For Lesbian and Gay Couples. 13th edition.* Berkeley: NOLO

3. Metcalfe, G. (2005, April 1). Gay Adoption. In *Florida Bar News.* 33(7) p. 2.

4. Rostow, A. (2005, January 10). High Courts Ignores Gay Adoption Appeal. In *The Advocate News and Politics.* URL [On-line] www.planetout.com

5. Patterson, C.J. (2004a). Lesbian and gay parents and their children: Summary of research findings. In *Lesbian and gay parenting: A resource for psychologists.* Washington, DC: American Psychological Association.

6. Armesto, J. C. (2002). Developmental and contextual factors that influence gay fathers' parental competence: A review of the literature. *Psychology of Men and Masculinity, 3,* 67-78.

7. Paige, R. U. (2004). Proceedings of the American Psychological Association, Incorporated, for the legislative year 2004. Minutes of the meeting of the Council of Representatives July 28 & 30, 2004. *American Psychologists.* 60, 5 www.apa.org/governance

8. Human Rights Campaign. (2006). Iowa Legislation / Ballot Initiative. Non-Discrimination: *Iowa S.B. 126/H.B. 596.* URL [On-line] www.hrc.org/takeaction/lawsandlegislationinyourstate.htm

9. Human Rights Campaign. (2006). Iowa Legislation / Ballot Initiative. *Safe Schools: Iowa H.S.B. 220/S.S.B 1160/S.S.B. 1308, S.F. 150.* URL [On-line] www.hrc.org/takeaction/lawsandlegislationinyourstate.htm

10. Human Rights Campaign. (2006). Florida Legislation / Ballot Initiative. *Safe Schools: Florida H.B. 87.* URL [On-line] www.hrc.org/takeaction/lawsandlegislationinyourstate.htm

11. Sloan, L., King, L. Sheppard, S. (1998). Hate Crimes Motivated by Sexual Orientation. In L. Sloan, N. Gristavsson (eds) *Violence and Social Injustice Against Lesbians, Gays, and Bisexual People.* Binghamton: Harrington Park Press.

12. Human Rights Campaign. (2006). *Statewide Hate Crime Laws.* URL [On-line] www.hrc.org/takeaction/lawsandlegislationinyourstate.htm

13. Murphy, B.C. (1994). Difference and Diversity: Gay and Lesbian Couple. In L. Kurdek (ed.) *Social Services for Gay and Lesbian Couples.* Binghamton: Haworth Press.

14. Human Rights Campaign. (2006). *Immigration.* URL [On-line] www.hrc.org/takeaction/issues/immigration.htm

15. United States General Accounting Office. (1997, January 31). Table of Statutory Provision Involving Marital Statutes to the United States Code. *Defense of Marriage Act GAO/OGC-97-16.* Washington D.C.

16. Human Rights Campaign. (2006). Rhode Island Legislation / Ballot Initiative. *Rhode Island H.B. 6925/S.B. 2149*. URL [On-line] www.hrc.org/takeaction/lawsandlegislationinyourstate.htm

17. Human Rights Campaign. (2006*). States Prohibitions on Marriage for Same Sex Couples*. URL [On-line] www.hrc.org/takeaction/lawsandlegislationinyourstate.htm

18. Human Rights Campaign. (2006). *Lobbying: The Heart of American Democracy*. URL. [On-line] http://www.hrcactioncenter.org/actioncenter/lobby_marriage.html

19. Faderman, L. (2000). *To Believe in Women: What Lesbians Have Done for America-A History*. New York: Houghton Mufflin.

978-0-595-45696-3
0-595-45696-0

www.ingramcontent.com/pod-product-compliance
Lightning Source LLC
Chambersburg PA
CBHW051422280526
45785CB00003B/1130